ANCIENT CULTURE AND SOCIETY

AUGUSTUS

ANCIENT CULTURE AND SOCIETY

General Editor
M. I. FINLEY

Professor of Ancient History
at the University of Cambridge

Other titles in preparation

AUGUSTUS

A. H. M. JONES

*Late Professor of Ancient History
at the University of Cambridge*

W · W · NORTON & COMPANY · INC · NEW YORK

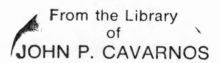

From the Library
of
JOHN P. CAVARNOS

SBN 393 04328 2   CLOTH EDITION
SBN 393 00584 4   PAPER EDITION

CONTENTS

GENEALOGICAL TABLE

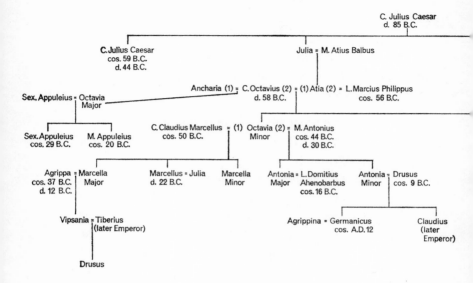

The Main Events of Augustus' Life and Reign

63 B.C.	Birth of Octavius	40 B.C.	Antonius marries Octavia
59 B.C.	Consulship of Caesar		Herod declared King
58–49 B.C.	Caesar proconsul of Gaul	39–38 B.C.	Parthians repulsed
58 B.C.	Death of Octavius' father	39 B.C.	Treaty of Misenum
46–44 B.C.	Caesar's dictatorship	38 B.C.	Octavian marries Livia
44 B.C.	Octavius' adoption Caesar assassinated	38–36 B.C.	War with Sextus Pompeius
43 B.C.	Battle of Mutina Octavian Consul I	36 B.C.	Defeat of Sextus Pompeius and Lepidus
43–33 B.C.	Triumvirate		Antonius' Parthian expedition
42 B.C.	Battle of Philippi		
41–40 B.C.	War of Perusia Parthian Invasion	35–34 B.C.	Dalmatian War
40 B.C.	Treaty of Brundisium	34 B.C.	Antonius annexes Armenia

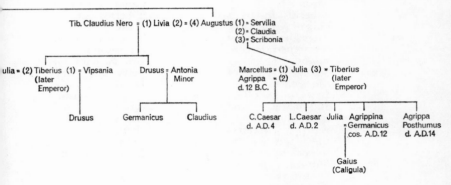

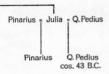

Pinarius = Julia = Q. Pedius

Pinarius   Q. Pedius
cos. 43 B.C.

Tib. Claudius Nero = (1) Livia (2) = (4) Augustus (1) = Servilia
(2) = Claudia
(3) = Scribonia

ulia = (2) Tiberius (1) = Vipsania   Drusus = Antonia
(later   Minor
Emperor)

Marcellus = (1) Julia (3) = Tiberius
Agrippa = (2)   (later
d. 12 B.C.   Emperor)

Drusus   Germanicus   Claudius

C. Caesar   L. Caesar   Julia   Agrippina   Agrippa
d. A.D. 4   d. A.D. 2   = Germanicus   Posthumus
                                cos. A.D. 12   d. A.D. 14

Gaius
(Caligula)

33 B.C.	Octavian consul II		the name Augustus
32 B.C.	Antonius divorces Octavia	26–24 B.C.	Augustus consul VIII–X
	Oath of allegiance		Augustus in Spain
31 B.C.	Octavian consul III		The first prefect of the city
	Battle of Actium		
30 B.C.	Octavian consul IV	25 B.C.	Expedition of Aelius Gallus to Arabia
	Death of Antonius and Cleopatra		Ethiopian war
	Annexation of Egypt		Annexation of Galatia
29 B.C.	Octavian consul V	23 B.C.	Augustus resigns his consulship (XI) and receives the tribunician power
	His triple triumph		
28 B.C.	Octavian consul VI		
	His first census and purge of the Senate		
27 B.C.	Octavian consul VII		Agrippa receives the proconsular *imperium* for five years
	He restores the Republic and receives		

THE MAIN EVENTS

THE MAIN EVENTS

PREFACE

THIS book has been greatly improved by the constructive criticism of the general editor of the series, Dr M. I. Finley of Jesus College, Cambridge, and of Dr John M. Moore of Radley College, who represented the schoolmaster's interest. I took most of their advice, but on one important issue I stood my ground, and in justice to them I should shoulder the blame if I was wrong. They wanted me to arrange the book on the conventional scheme followed, for instance, by *The Cambridge Ancient History*, a narrative up to Actium, and then a treatment by topics—the constitution, the provinces, the army, etc. I preferred to put all the major developments into the main narrative, and to add a number of short chapters on matters which did not easily fall into the chronological framework. This method admittedly makes more difficult reading, but the other falsifies reality, in which constitutional changes, wars, administrative revisions were closely interlocked.

On one point I reluctantly yielded to the pressure of my advisers—to call the hero of the book Octavian between 43 and 27 B.C. He was of course always called Caesar by all his contemporaries (except Brutus, who rudely called him Octavius, as if he had never been adopted). The point is not merely pedantic; his rise to power depended greatly on his being Caesar. However, Dr Finley and Dr Moore were firm that my readers would find it difficult to distinguish Caesar the dictator from Caesar his adopted son, and I accepted their verdict.

A. H. M. J.

NOTE

Shortly before his sudden death on the 9th April 1970, Professor Jones completed, with the exception of the index, the final details in preparing this volume for publication. Everything is therefore exactly as he wanted it.

M. I. F.

The Breakdown of the Republic

THE breakdown of the Roman Republic has been called
Hannibal's legacy, and there is some truth in the epigram.
The long years (218–201 B.C.) of fighting and ravaging up and
down Italy, and the long years of military service at home
and abroad, impoverished the peasantry and brought many
of them to ruin. In the years that followed, the Spanish provinces acquired during the war meant more long-term service
abroad, while the Eastern wars brought in a flood of money,
most of which found its way into the pockets of the upper
classes, particularly senators. Their inevitable reaction was
to invest this money in land and, since the wars produced a
glut of slaves, to stock their new estates with slaves. The
peasant proprietors began to be squeezed out, and a rural
proletariat of landless peasants began to form. These were
the origins of the agrarian problem which was to dog the
Roman Republic for the rest of its existence.

The second Punic war, and still more the wars overseas
which followed it, also embittered relations between Rome
and her Italian allies. The cities and tribes of Italy, as they
had one by one been subdued, had been given treaties, under
which they were obliged to supply troops to fight in Rome's
wars. As long as these wars were in Italy, against such common enemies as the Gauls, the allies felt no particular grievance. But now that they had to fight to win provinces or
indemnities for the sole benefit of Rome, they began to be
restive. Roman magistrates and the Senate had, moreover, in
the period of the second Punic war grown used to ordering
the allies about in an arbitrary fashion, and continued to
do so in peace time.

It was the agrarian problem that sparked off the violence
that was ultimately to destroy the Republic. Tiberius Gracchus' bill, enacted in 133 B.C. for distributing the public land,
after leaving a generous allowance to the occupiers, in small
lots to poor citizens, excited such furious resistance among the

senatorial landowners that a group of them lynched Gracchus. This was the first of a series of violent clashes between two groups who called themselves the *optimates* and the *populares*. The nucleus of the *optimates* was the small clique of nobles (men whose fathers, grandfathers or more remote ancestors had been consuls) who more or less monopolized the highest offices and dominated the Senate, but they had wide support among the propertied class, even, as Cicero says, prosperous freedmen; otherwise they could not have maintained their unbroken hold on the higher magistracies. They were conservatives, who regarded the rights of property as sacred, and therefore resisted bitterly any attempts to redistribute land or cancel debt. They were upholders of the constitution and of religion, which could be used to block any revolutionary legislation. Though at times they had to yield to popular pressure, they always remained the government.

The *populares* were a much less well defined group. Their leaders were individual politicians or very small groups of politicians, who at intervals attempted to legislate in the interests of the people, by which they meant the common people. Most of them were also nobles, and their usual weapon was the tribunate of the plebs, which was the normal legislative office—when the Senate wanted a law passed it normally requested the tribunes to put it to the plebeian assembly, and a tribune could pass a law without the assent of the Senate—and possessed other formidable powers, such as an all embracing veto and the right of impeaching the most senior magistrates (after their year of office) before the people: it was also an office to which it was easy to be elected, since there were ten tribunes a year. The *populares* developed a regular programme of legislation. First came the distribution of smallholdings to landless citizens. These were at first offered to all. Later, when Marius began to recruit landless peasants into the army, the distribution was limited to time-served soldiers, who obviously had a superior claim. The next point in the programme was the provision by the state of corn for the proletariat of Rome at a price that they could afford. From time to time the *populares* were interested in the problem of debt, which frequently meant agricultural indebtedness. They were early successful in introducing the

2

secret ballot into voting in the assembly, for legislation, elections and trials. They also stood up against the execution of Roman citizens without a lawful trial; the Senate was very prone to ignore this elementary right of the citizen in what it deemed to be political crises. Most *populares* advocated the grant of the citizenship to the Italian allies. They were generally interested in the welfare of the provincials; most of the extortion laws were promoted by *populares*. Finally they substituted *equites* (citizens owning 400,000 sesterces who were not senators) for senators as jurors in the criminal courts.

Support came to the *populares* from different sections of the population according to the measures that they advocated from time to time. The landless peasants flocked to Rome to vote for land allotments, but the urban poor were more interested in distribution of corn. It was the peasant proprietors who clamoured for abolition of debt. The *equites* were uncertain in their allegiance. They would support a popular leader who championed their control of the criminal courts, but the thought of distribution of land or abolition of debt promptly sent them into the camp of the *optimates*. Apart from the allies themselves, who having no votes were politically valueless, no one favoured their enfranchisement; for one reason or another *optimates*, the *equites*, the urban proletariat and the peasantry were opposed to it. We know the fact but we can only infer the reasons. In general there was a reluctance to extend and thereby dilute the privileges of citizenship. The nobles no doubt feared that the aristocratic families in the Italian cities would break their monopoly of high office at Rome. The *equites* may have feared that wealthy Italian groups would outbid them for the tax contracts and compete for the equestrian militiae, the officer-posts of prefect and tribune in the army. The urban proletariat may have feared that poor Italians would migrate to Rome and compete for the wheat ration, the peasants that they would apply for land allotments.

Tribunes might every now and then pass laws through the *concilium plebis*, where rich and poor were evenly distributed over the thirty-five tribes and the vote was thus controlled by the lower classes, but the Senate was the permanent governing body of Rome, and the Senate was dominated by its senior

3

members, the ex-consuls. The *populares* were never able to gain control of the government except in the revolutionary situation of 87–82 B.C. They rarely achieved the consulship or even the praetorship, as the *optimates* always retained the control of the *comitia centuriata*.

In this assembly the 18 centuries of *equites* and the 70 centuries of the first (wealthiest) class almost had a majority of the 193 votes. There was a natural affinity of interests and sentiment between these voters and the *optimates*; both were wealthy and tended to be conservative. The nobles, moreover, as consuls and proconsuls, praetors and propraetors, had the *equestres militiae,* much prized offices, in their gift. The equestrian and first class centuries were moreover small, that is had relatively few voters in each, and each voter was therefore worth bribing. It is certain that there was bribery in the consular elections on a scale which only *optimates* could afford.

The *populares* thus never gained substantial representation in the Senate, much less a majority. They had to be content to remain a permanent opposition, occasionally forcing through individual measures in the teeth of the Senate.

Up to 91 B.C. the political struggles of the Republic were no more than sanguinary riots, followed by savage reprisals by the Senate. In 91 the Italian allies, driven to desperation by the murder of the tribune Drusus on the eve of the poll for his bill for their enfranchisement, broke into armed revolt. The bulk of the allies accepted the Roman offer of the franchise to all who laid down their arms forthwith, but a substantial block, comprising the Samnites and the other highland tribes, fought on, and a bitter and bloody war ensued, which ended in the surrender of most of the rebels in 87 B.C.; the Samnites were not finally crushed until 82 B.C. This was not technically a civil war, since the allies were foreigners and not citizens, but since they were fighting not for independence but for citizenship, it had the emotional impact of a civil war.

A real civil war soon followed. The senate tried to restrict the franchise of the new Italian citizens, a popular tribune Sulpicius proposed a bill to give the Italians full voting rights, but realized that if he was to get it through against the opposition of the optimate consuls, Pompeius and Sulla, he must gain the support of Marius and his thousands of veterans. One of the effects of Marius' recruiting policy had been greatly to strengthen the hold which a commander had over his men, both in service and after. The landless peasants who formed the bulk of the armies knew that they depended on their commander to get them the smallholdings that they craved— the Senate automatically blocked any land bill—and they therefore gave him their political support. Marius' veterans had already made themselves useful not only by their votes, but by terrorizing magistrates who tried to use obstructive tactics.

Unfortunately Marius' terms were the transfer to himself from Sulla, the consul who had lawfully drawn the province, of the command in the Mithradatic war. Sulla, who was at Nola with his army, which had already fought in the Social war under his command, appealed to them to protect his rights. His officers deserted him, but the men clamoured to march on Rome. Sulla easily occupied Rome, reversed Sulpicius' laws, passed a few laws designed to confirm the dominance of the Senate, and proscribed twelve of his principal opponents.

This was the first occasion on which a Roman magistrate secured control of the government by means of a regular Roman army, and incidentally the first on which a political leader killed his opponents without any form of trial. But two could play at this game, and as soon as Sulla had left for the East, the leaders of the *populares* marched their armies on Rome, proscribed their opponents and seized the government. Five years later Sulla returned with his veteran army, crushed the armies of the state, held a huge proscription, and had himself elected dictator without time limit and with unlimited powers.

Caesar later said that Sulla did not know his alphabet when he resigned his dictatorship (Suetonius, *Iulius* 77). But Sulla was a convinced optimate and had no taste for the boring task of government. He accordingly tried to revive the old Republic to which all *optimates* looked back with nostalgia. He reduced the tribunate of the plebs to complete impotence, he regulated the *cursus honorum* so that no one should reach high office—and the command of an army—until mature age, and he strengthened the Senate, doubling its size by adding 300 loyal *equites*. This does not seem to have been a happy move. The new members had not the unyielding optimate principles of the old senatorial families, and made a number of halfhearted concessions to tribunician agitation.

The real danger was however no longer the tribunes but ambitious men who saw the opportunity of gaining glory, influence and power by the control of armies. Most of these men adopted the label of *populares,* but very few were genuinely interested in the popular programme. A notable exception is Julius Caesar, who had a passionate interest in land distribution, not only to veterans—Pompeius' and his own—but to the urban proletariat of Rome, 20,000 of whom he planted in Campania during his consulship and 80,000 in overseas colonies during his dictatorship. The others professed popular sympathies with personal ends in view. They wanted larger provinces, bigger armies, more money and longer terms of office than the Senate was willing to concede, and these could only be got by a law passed by a popular tribune. The career of Pompeius is a striking illustration. He started as an optimate, raising a private army in support of Sulla in 83 B.C. at the age of twenty-three. When the retiring consul Lepidus, a *popularis,* raised a rebellion in 77 B.C. Pompeius was given a command under Lepidus' optimate colleague Catulus, and having troops under his command blackmailed the Senate into sending him as proconsul to Spain to crush the popular leader Sertorius. Returning from this campaign in 70 B.C. with a large army he again blackmailed the Senate into allowing him to be, contrary to every rule of the constitution, a candidate for the consulate—and abruptly became a *popularis* and restored the tribunate.

The tribunate became very useful to him three years later when Gabinius, tribune of the plebs, passed a law in the teeth of the Senate giving him a three-year command over the whole Mediterranean to curb the pirates. Next year another popular tribune, Manilius, gave him even more extensive powers to finish off the Mithradatic war. Thereafter such extraordinary commands, always created by tribunicial laws, became increasingly common. It has been urged that they

THE BREAKDOWN OF THE REPUBLIC

were required by the abnormal strategic needs of the time. The *lex Gabinia* might be so justified; a campaign against the pirates required special powers and resources. But the Senate could perfectly well have provided them, and had done so in 74 B.C., when it gave the praetor Marcus Antonius a territorially unlimited command (*imperium infinitum*) and kept him in it for three years. There was no strategical need to give extraordinary powers to Pompeius for the Mithradatic war, still less to Caesar in Gaul in 59, Piso and Gabinius in Macedonia and Syria in 58, Pompeius and Crassus in Spain and Syria in 55. Finally there came a clash between two great commanders, each with a large army devoted to its leader. Caesar, a *popularis* detested and dreaded by the *optimates*, held the Gauls, Pompeius, by now an optimate again and jealous of Caesar's glory, held the Spains. The *optimates* and Pompeius were determined to break Caesar's career, Caesar was equally determined to have his second consulate. So it came to civil war and Caesar won, and like Sulla became dictator, but unlike Sulla did not resign. The Republic was finished.

It is difficult to see how it could have been revived. The authority of the Senate had collapsed. The old habit whereby magistrates and promagistrates obeyed its instructions no longer prevailed. Armies obeyed the orders of their commanders, even to fight the government of Rome. Sulla had tried to strengthen the Senate, but it became weaker than ever. He had tried to keep military commands in the hands of senior men, and to make them annual, but despite all his restrictive measures the tribunate of the plebs had been revived, and used to create extraordinary commands. A possible remedy might have been to have gone back to the pre-Marian army, and conscript unwilling freeholders, who would not have supported their commanders in civil wars. Another remedy might have been for the state to supply land allotments for discharged soldiers, who would not wish to jeopardize them by rebellion. Neither remedy was suggested. The first would have been very unpopular among small landowners. The second would have been enormously expensive, probably requiring direct taxation of citizens. Augustus found a solution in his restored Republic, but it was not a Republic.

Caesar's Heir

GAIUS OCTAVIUS was born at Rome on 24 September in the consulship of Cicero and Antonius (63 B.C.). The Octavii were an old and wealthy family of Velitrae, a little town some twenty-five miles southeast of Rome. Locally they were no doubt respected, but until recently they had not been ambitious. Gaius' grandfather, Gaius Octavius, had been a member of the equestrian order, a banker. It was his father, another Gaius Octavius, who first aspired to and achieved senatorial rank. As a young man he served twice as military tribune, and then, probably about 70 B.C., was elected quaestor, thus entering the Senate. About five years later he married a second time. Of his first wife, Ancharia, we know nothing except that she bore him a daughter, Octavia (Major). His second match with Atia was evidence of his rising importance, and an aid to his political career. On her father's side, it is true, his bride's ancestry was no more than respectable: the Atii Balbi were the leading family of a neighbouring little town, Aricia, and though of senatorial rank for several generations had never risen above the praetorship. But Atia's mother, Julia, belonged to the very blueblooded patrician family of the Julii Caesares, and was the sister of Gaius Julius Caesar, a daring left wing politician who was making his mark in Rome.

In 65 B.C. Julius Caesar was curule aedile, and made himself immensely popular by the extravagant splendour of his games. It was probably in this year that Gaius Octavius was elected plebeian aedile. After his aedileship, according to the regular routine he presided over one of the criminal courts. Then in 62 B.C., the year of Julius Caesar's praetorship, he was elected praetor for the following year at the top of the poll. During his praetorship he won a eulogy from Cicero for the combination of courtesy and firmness with which he handled highly contentious cases—claims for restitution brought by victims of the Sullan regime. In the allotment of provinces he obtained Macedonia, which he governed with success for two years, winning some military victories for which he was saluted *imperator*, and displaying tact and firmness in civil affairs. He might now reasonably have hoped for the consulship, but returning from Macedonia he died before he could become a candidate.

Atia had borne him two children, Octavia (Minor) and Gaius, who was four when his father died. She was soon married again, to a really aristocratic husband, Lucius Marcius Philippus, who shortly afterwards held the consulate in 56 B.C. He was a very cautious man, who despite his high rank managed to avoid taking sides in the acute political controversies of the day. He was a good stepfather to Gaius, and between them he and Atia gave him a sound rather old-fashioned education.

Gaius made his first public appearance at the age of eleven when, as her sole male descendant, he delivered a funeral oration on his grandmother Julia. He no doubt studied the funeral oration which his great-uncle had delivered for his aunt Julia nearly twenty years before, and like him recalled the divine descent of the Iulii from Iulus, the son of Aeneas, the son of Anchises and Venus. One may also imagine that he heard with excitement of Caesar's conquests in Gaul and his invasion of Britain and Germany, and that his great-uncle became something of a hero to him.

Caesar had not as yet produced a son, and his only daughter had died childless in 55 B.C. His nearest relatives were three great-nephews, the two grandsons of his eldest sister, Lucius Pinarius and Quintus Pedius, and the grandson of his second sister, Gaius Octavius. He is not recorded to have taken any interest in Pinarius, except that he ultimately remembered him in his will. In 58 B.C. he took Pedius, who was considerably older than Octavius, with him as one of his legates to Gaul, where he stayed two or three years. On his return to Rome in 49 he got Pedius elected praetor, and in 46 he sent him as one of his legates to Spain to open operations against the two sons of Pompeius. Pedius fought in the campaign of Munda and was on his return allowed a triumph. Despite these favours, Caesar was evidently not impressed by Pedius' abilities.

9

To Gaius Octavius, on the other hand, he showed a marked preference. It is not certain when he first saw the boy, but perhaps not until he returned to Rome from the East in September 47, after having defeated Pompeius at Pharsalus. Though Octavius was only just sixteen, Caesar had him elected to a vacancy in the college of the *pontifices,* and invited him to join his staff for the forthcoming campaign against the Pompeians in Africa. Atia vetoed this proposal, saying that Octavius was too young, but to console him for his disappointment Caesar on his return from his victorious campaign gave Octavius military decorations and allowed him to march in his triumph. He also made use of the power recently granted by a *lex Cassia* to enrol Octavius among the ancient and hitherto strictly hereditary aristocracy of Rome, the patricians, and appointed him to preside over some of the games he gave that summer. The strain proved too much for Octavius, who was a delicate boy, and he fell ill just as Caesar was preparing to march for Spain against the sons of Pompeius. Caesar told him to get well quickly and follow as soon as he could. Octavius took him at his word and after an adventurous journey, including a shipwreck, caught up with his great-uncle in southern Spain, but, alas, not until after the battle of Munda had been fought and won (17 March 46). Caesar was pleased with his enterprise and pluck, and kept him with him until he returned to Rome in October.

Caesar's next campaigns, now that the civil wars against the Pompeians and Republicans were over, were to be against the Dacians, north of the Danube, and then against the Parthians, and six legions were concentrated in Macedonia. Caesar agreed to take Octavius on his staff, and apparently nominated him to be his *magister equitum* for the campaign. Meanwhile he sent him across to Macedonia, to spend the winter at Apollonia, a Greek city on the Adriatic coast south of Dyrrachium, where he was to complete his literary education under the distinguished Greek rhetorician, Apollodorus of Pergamum, and at the same time receive military training from the officers of the legions stationed nearby. Octavius took with him some of his own friends, including a schoolfellow of humble origins, Marcus Vipanius Agrippa, and he made friends among the junior officers, among them Quintus Salvidienus Rufus, who had started life as a shepherd.

Octavius had been at Apollonia for a little over three months, when one evening late in March a freedman of his mother arrived, bringing a letter from her. She wrote that Caesar had been murdered in the senate house by Brutus and Cassius and others, and urged him to come home at once; the future was uncertain. The freedman who had brought the letter could add little, as he had started immediately after the murder and travelled at full speed, ahead of the news, but he thought that any relative of Caesar's would be in danger from the conspirators, who were a powerful group. Some centurions said that if he appealed to the troops, they would guarantee to rally their men to him, and Agrippa and Salvidienus strongly recommended this course. But Octavius felt he was too young and inexperienced to risk such a perilous venture. The leading citizens of Apollonia offered him the protection of their city. But Octavius decided to take his mother's advice, and took ship across the Adriatic. He did not sail for Brundisium, where he was afraid that a watch might be kept for him, but for the open shore some twenty miles further south, whence he walked to the little town of Lupiae. Here he heard more news. Marcus Antonius, Caesar's colleague as consul, had agreed to an amnesty with Caesar's murderers, but the Roman people had burnt Caesar's corpse in the Forum and chased his murderers out of town and burnt their houses. But the most exciting news of all was that Caesar's will had been opened, and that Octavius had been named heir to three-quarters of his estate (the other quarter being divided between his cousins Pinarius and Pedius), and finally that he had been adopted as his son.

It was now clear that he was in no personal danger—in point of fact he never had been, for the tyrannicides were high-minded men who had no intention of killing anyone except the tyrant himself—and he entered Brundisium. Here he picked up more letters from his mother again begging him to hurry home, and from his stepfather, Philippus, strongly urging him not to accept the inheritance and the adoption with all their dangers, but to content himself with a quiet life. Octavius wrote back that he wanted to accept. Philippus

continued to disagree, but Atia, torn between fear and ambition for her son, eventually gave way. Having consulted other
friends, Octavius made up his mind to accept, and from henceforth called himself no longer Gaius Octavius, but Gaius
Julius Caesar. He might have taken the additional name
Octavianus, but never did, preferring to identify himself completely with his adoptive father. He will nevertheless be called
Octavian for the rest of this chapter and the next to avoid
confusion with the dictator.

He travelled slowly up to Rome. The towns he passed
through did not all welcome him, but everywhere he was
enthusiastically greeted by his adoptive father's veterans, who
thronged up from their colonies to welcome him. On 18 April
44 B.C., he reached Naples and the next day met Cornelius
Balbus, the able Spaniard from Gades who had been Caesar's
confidential man of business. He soon rejoined his stepfather
and mother at their villa near Cumae, and Philippus introduced him to the neighbours, among them Cicero:

> Octavius was with me here; very complimentary and very
> friendly. His friends called him Caesar, but Philippus did
> not, and so I did not either. I say he cannot be a good
> citizen; there are so many people about him who threaten
> our friends with death. They say the situation is intoler-
> able. What do you think, when the boy comes to Rome,
> where our liberators cannot be safe? (Cicero, *Letters to
> Atticus*, XIV, 12, 2).

Cicero was quite right in distrusting Octavian. We do not
of course know what was going on inside his mind at this
time, but one can make a fair guess. He must have felt a
furious hatred for the murderers of his beloved and idolized
great-uncle from the first, but when he learnt that he was his
son it became his sacred duty to exact vengeance from them.
When first he heard the news he must have been bitterly dis-
appointed at being robbed of the hopes of a brilliant career
under Caesar's patronage. Now he felt it to be his sacred
mission to follow in his father's footsteps.

He was, however, fully aware that he would have to be
very discreet at first if he was to achieve his purposes. It was
obvious already that as Caesar's favourite kinsman and still

more as Caesar's son he commanded enthusiastic support from soldiers and veterans, who seem to have been embarrassingly eager for him to lead them against Caesar's murderers. Caesar's equestrian friends, his bankers and men of affairs, men like Balbus and Oppius, Matius, Sasenna and Rabirius Postumus, also rallied to him, and provided him with ample financial backing. But to build up political support was a much more difficult matter. The political situation was very unstable. On one extreme were the supporters of the tyrannicides, amongst whom Cicero was the most eminent figure; on the other extreme, Caesar's men, led by Marcus Antonius, who had the people and the majority of the tribunes behind them; in the middle were the moderates, whose chief aim was to avoid another civil war. Antonius had hitherto pursued a fairly moderate policy, but about this time (the end of April) made an alarming move. He had earlier in the year received Macedonia as his consular province. He now announced that he intended to ask the Senate on 1 June to let him exchange it for Cisalpine Gaul and Gallia Comata and to extend his term, and that of his colleague Dolabella in Syria, to five years. This was suspiciously like the province which Julius Caesar had used as a base for making himself dictator. Directly after this Antonius left Rome for Campania to establish more colonies for veterans. He took the opportunity to tour all the colonies of the region, and to get the veterans to swear to maintain Caesar's acts, and to instruct the magistrates of the colonies to establish stocks of arms.

Octavian moved on to Rome early in May and promptly approached the praetor Gaius Antonius, Marcus Antonius' brother, and formally took up the inheritance. When Marcus Antonius returned from Campania, escorted by a large body of veterans, Octavian called on him. He had two requests to make. A formal meeting of the *comitia curiata* was required to make his adoption legally valid; would Antonius arrange it? Secondly, while Octavian had obtained legal possession of Caesar's land and house property, he had not got his liquid assets, for Caesar's widow Calpurnia had handed over to Antonius not only her late husband's papers, but all his cash, amounting, it was said, to nearly 100 million sesterces (25 million denarii). Under the will the heirs had to pay a legacy

13

of 300 sesterces (75 denarii) to every Roman citizen; this meant only the urban plebs which received the corn dole, but they numbered 250,000, so that 75 million sesterces (18,750,000 denarii) was immediately required.

Antonius could hardly refuse the *lex curiata,* though he later had it blocked by tribunes, but he would not part with the money, alleging apparently that most of the sum he had received from Calpurnia was public funds. This may have been true, but it was probably also true that Antonius had spent the money already. Throughout the interview Antonius was unhelpful and even hostile.

It is rather difficult to say why he took this line. He can hardly have regarded a young man of eighteen as a serious political rival even if he was Caesar's heir; and if he had appreciated his potentialities, he would have been wiser to win him over to his side. It has been suggested that he feared that Octavian might pursue an aggressive policy and break up the compromise with the opposition which he had at first maintained. But Antonius seems to have already abandoned this moderate policy, and once again his wisest policy would have been to make himself Octavian's political mentor. It seems likeliest that Antonius had been irritated at Caesar's favouritism towards an obscure young relative and acted out of bad temper.

Octavian, who had imagined that Antonius, his adoptive father's greatest friend, would receive him with open arms, was bitterly chagrined at his insulting reception. He responded by ostentatiously beginning to auction his adoptive father's property, and even some of his own, and from the proceeds to pay out the legacies to the plebs, thus winning vast popularity for himself and throwing odium on Antonius. He also demanded that Caesar's golden throne, which the Senate had decreed should be displayed at all public games, should be so displayed at the *ludi Cereales.* This demand was resisted by Antonius, and ultimately vetoed by some tribunes, but Octavian was able to make political capital out of the incident.

When 1 June came the proposed change in the consular provinces was not brought up in the Senate: evidently Antonius realized that there would be too much opposition.

Instead a few days later a plebiscite was passed, without due notice being given, enacting the exchange of provinces and furthermore empowering Antonius to transfer the six legions in Macedonia to Gaul.

Octavian continued his campaign of winning popularity by undertaking to celebrate at his own expense (assisted by three of his adoptive father's financier friends) the games in honour of Venus Genetrix which Caesar had instituted, but which had been dropped after his death. He celebrated them with great splendour from 20 to 30 July, and again tried to display Caesar's golden throne, and was again prevented by Antonius. Fortune aided him, for by a lucky coincidence a comet appeared. 'On the very days of my games,' he wrote in his autobiography (quoted in Pliny, *Natural History* II, 93):

a comet was seen in the northern part of the sky for seven days. It appeared about the eleventh hour of the day and was clearly visible in all countries. The people believed that by that star it was signified that the soul of Caesar was received among the immortal gods, on which account the sign of a star was attached to the head of the statue of Caesar which I shortly consecrated in the Forum.

This was the interpretation which he publicly accepted, but privately we are told that he believed that the star 'was born for him and he was born in it'.

The veterans who formed Antonius' unofficial bodyguard in Rome became more and more shocked at the bitter feud between Antonius, Caesar's greatest friend, and Caesar's son and heir, and eventually they sent a deputation to Antonius urging him to drop the quarrel. Antonius could hardly refuse, and it was arranged that he should go to the Capitol, and that Octavian should be brought to him there. A public reconciliation was then celebrated in the presence of the veterans.

Meanwhile the political situation had been deteriorating. It had been hoped that at a meeting of the Senate on 1 August Antonius would make some concession, perhaps even give up the Gallic provinces, and that something might be done for Brutus and Cassius, who wanted provinces allotted to them since they could not be safe at Rome. But nothing came of these hopes. Calpurnius Piso, Julius Caesar's father-in-law, made an attack on Antonius in the Senate, but no one ventured to support him. Brutus and Cassius, after an acrimonious exchange of letters and edicts with Antonius, sailed for the East, having been voted two minimal provinces, Crete and Cyrene. On 1 September Antonius made a violent attack on Cicero for failing to attend the Senate, and next day Cicero replied with a temperate criticism of Antonius' policy. Antonius replied with a savage invective on 19 September and on 2 October denounced the assassins of Caesar in a popular assembly. A few days later he arrested some of his veterans on the charge of trying to assassinate him, and when Octavian offered him the services of his own bodyguard, rudely rejected the offer and let it be known that he suspected Octavian himself of being the instigator of the attempted assassination. A few days later, on 9 October, he left for Brundisium to meet the Macedonian legions which he had ordered to cross and proceed to Cisalpine Gaul.

It was, it would seem, believed by many that Antonius would march his legions on Rome, in which case Octavian could fear the worst. He determined to try to win over the Macedonian legions, to which he was personally known, and sent agents down to Brundisium with bundles of pamphlets. He also determined on a bolder step, to raise a private army from his adoptive father's veterans. Accompanied by a group of supporters, including Marcus Agrippa, his old schoolmate, and Gaius Maecenas, a wealthy Etruscan of ancient family, he set off for Campania with some cartloads of money. What happened next may be told in Cicero's words (Cicero, *Letters to Atticus* XIV, 8, 1–2):

On the evening of the 1st I had a letter from Octavianus. He is doing great things. He won over to his side the veterans at Casilinum and Calatia. No wonder, he is giving them 500 denarii each. He is thinking of going round the other colonies. Clearly this means that there will be war against Antonius with him as leader. Which are we to follow? Look at his name and his age. He asks me if he can have a secret conference with me here or at Capua. It is childish, if he thinks that it can be done secretly. I have

16

told him in a letter that it is neither necessary nor possible. He has sent me one Caecina of Volaterrae, a friend of his, with the message that Antonius is marching on the city with the legion of the Alaudae, is demanding money from the towns, is leading his legion with colours flying. He asked whether he should march to Rome with his 3000 veterans, or hold Capua and bar Antonius' advance, or go to the three Macedonian legions, which are marching along the Adriatic coast, which he hopes are on his side. They refused to accept a donative from Antonius, according to Caecina, and showered abuse on him and would not listen when he made a speech to them.

Octavian was anxious that his illegal coup should receive some official recognition, and kept begging Cicero to come to Rome and save the Republic a second time; could not the Senate be summoned? Cicero advised him to go to Rome, but refused to involve himself in a wildcat adventure under a leader whom he did not trust. So when he arrived with his veterans at Rome Octavian had to be content with addressing the people; Cannutius, a tribune very hostile to Antonius, summoned a meeting for him. When news came of Antonius' return, many of Caesar's veterans declared they would not fight him, and Octavian thought it best to march them into Etruria. Here he established a base at Arretium and proceeded to recruit more men.

Antonius meanwhile had by drastic measures restored discipline in his legions and called a meeting of the Senate for 24 November. He failed to appear for unknown reasons, and called a second meeting for the 28th. It was rumoured that one of the senators was to denounce Octavian as a traitor, but when the day came Antonius only moved a vote of thanks to Lepidus, the proconsul of Hither Spain and Narbonese Gaul. He had persuaded Sextus Pompeius, the son of Pompeius Magnus, who had raised a revolt and conquered most of Further Spain, to submit on condition that he received compensation from the treasury for his father's enormous confiscated fortune of 700 million sesterces. The Senate met again in the evening and hurriedly carried through the allotment of the praetorian provinces for the coming year. The reason for these futile proceedings soon became known. One of the Macedonian legions, the Martia, had already mutinied, declared for Octavian—nominally for the Senate and people —and occupied Alba, and news had now come that another legion, the fourth, had followed suit.

Antonius must have regretted having gratuitously antagonized Octavian. He decided that there was nothing for it but to take command of his remaining legions, now only three in number, before any more deserted him, and to occupy his province. This he would not be able to do without a fight. The proconsul of Cisalpine Gaul was Decimus Brutus, one of Caesar's murderers, and early in December he issued a proclamation (Cicero, *Philippics* III, 8) that 'he would retain the province of Gaul in the power of the Senate and people of Rome'—despite Antonius' legal title to the province under the plebiscite of June. Hostilities soon began. Brutus had only three legions, one of which was of raw recruits, and he did not dare to venture these in battle against Antonius' three veteran legions. So he stocked Mutina with provisions and prepared to stand a siege until the Senate's forces should arrive.

At Rome nothing much could be done until the consuls of 43 B.C., Aulus Hirtius and Vibius Pansa, came into office on 1 January, but Cicero took advantage of a meeting of the Senate on 20 December to pass votes of thanks to Decimus Brutus and Octavian, thereby implicitly legalizing their actions. It is improbable that he now or later trusted in Octavian, but he was *de facto* in command of the only legions at the immediate disposal of the Senate—he had raised them to five, and the bulk of them were veterans—and Cicero therefore decided that he must try to keep him on the right side by honours and compliments and loudly affirm his loyalty to the Republic.

On 1 January and the three following days there was a prolonged and exacerbated debate in the Senate. Cicero wanted a state of emergency to be declared forthwith and Antonius declared a public enemy. Antonius' friends, backed by many moderates, carried a motion that three delegates should be sent to Antonius to present an ultimatum. It was, however, resolved that one of the consuls, Hirtius, should

18

proceed to the theatre of war, and that Pansa should hold levies throughout Italy. It was also voted, on Cicero's motion, that Octavian should be accorded *imperium pro praetore* and be made a senator, and that he might be a candidate for office as if he had already held the quaestorship, that is ten years in advance of the legal age. Octavian's stepfather also voted him an equestrian statue, and some other senator the right of speaking in the Senate among the consulars—Cicero had proposed among the praetorians. Octavian heard of these honours at Spoletium, and on 7 January, thereafter a red letter day in the Roman calendar, ceremonially inaugurated his *imperium*.

The delegates brought back Antonius' reply at the beginning of February. It was quite unacceptable and the Senate voted that the two consuls together with Octavian should see to it that the Republic took no harm. The first battle was fought on 15 April at Forum Gallorum, where after a murderous struggle Antonius was eventually defeated, but one of the consuls, Pansa, was seriously wounded. There followed a second battle on 21 April under the walls of Mutina. Antonius was decisively defeated, but the other consul Hirtius was killed; Pansa died a few days later.

Antonius did not venture another battle, but marched off westwards with the remnants of his army, intending to pick up three legions which his legate Ventidius had been recruiting in Italy, and then to try to win over Lepidus, who was encamped with his legions in southern Gaul. Aemilius Lepidus had been very close to Caesar. He had happened to be praetor in 49, the year that Caesar crossed the Rubicon, and had got him out of an awkward constitutional tangle by passing a law appointing him dictator, despite the absence of both consuls. He then went out to govern Hispania Citerior, recently recovered from Pompeius' legates, returning in 47 to celebrate a triumph and to be consul in 46. He succeeded Antonius as Caesar's *magister equitum* for 46–44, and virtually governed Italy during the dictator's frequent and prolonged absences on his campaigns. On Caesar's death he got himself elected *pontifex maximus* in his place, and withdrew to the large province which had been assigned to him by Caesar, Gallia Narbonensis and Hispania Citerior. He had hitherto sat on the fence, and advocated conciliation between Antonius and the Senate. But with his background he was more likely to support Antonius than to fight him.

Octavian took over the command of Pansa's four legions of recruits as well as his own five legions (some of which had been transferred to Hirtius' command). Decimus Brutus had an interview with Octavian and suggested that they should co-operate in crushing Antonius. He would himself pursue him up the Po valley along the via Aemilia, while Octavian would cross the Apennines and cut him off from Italy. Octavian apparently replied that he could not get his army to march; 'orders cannot be given to Caesar, and Caesar cannot give orders to his army; both very bad things', as Brutus later commented (Cicero, *Letters to his Friends,* XI, 10, 4). Brutus therefore set off two days after the battle with his own troops, who were in bad condition owing to the long siege.

Octavian's motives for his inactivity may be surmised. He cannot have liked the idea of co-operating with one of his adoptive father's murderers to crush Antonius, who, badly as he had treated him, had been Caesar's friend. Moreover, he was well aware that Cicero and his friends regarded him as a necessary instrument for the destruction of Antonius, to be discarded when that end was achieved. The Senate had already betrayed its feelings, when it heard of Antonius' defeat at Mutina, by awarding a triumph to Decimus Brutus but not even an ovation (proposed by Cicero) to himself, and by giving the command against Antonius to Brutus. He had since heard of a witticism of Cicero (*Letters to his Friends* XI, 20, 1), 'the young man is to be praised, honoured and exalted' (the last word might also mean 'removed'). If Antonius were crushed, there was a danger that the party of the murderers would gain the upper hand. Marcus Brutus had illegally occupied Macedonia and Illyricum, and early in February the Senate had regularized his position. Cassius had likewise illegally seized Syria, and was also recognized at the end of April. Moreover, as things stood, Decimus Brutus was consul designate with Munatius Plancus for the next year, and Marcus Brutus and Cassius would be consuls in 41 B.C. according to Caesar's *acta*, which the Senate had agreed to maintain. It seemed unlikely that in these circumstances

Octavian would be able to fulfil his design of taking vengeance on his father's murderers, or that he would win his
father's honours. His interests lay with the Caesarian party,
provided that he could win a leading place in it.

For this purpose, and for its own sake, he wanted the consulate, now vacant by the deaths of Hirtius and Pansa. It was
an outrageous ambition, seeing that he was only twenty, even
though he had been granted ten years' priority. He seems
nevertheless to have hoped to induce the Senate to grant the
necessary exemption spontaneously by a policy of masterly
inaction combined with propaganda by his supporters at
Rome.

Meanwhile the war against Antonius did not prosper.
Antonius effected a junction with Ventidius and his three
legions and pressed on to Gaul, while Decimus Brutus trailed
behind him, never succeeding in making contact. The Senate
instructed Octavian to send the two Macedonian legions, the
Martia and the fourth, to Brutus, but they refused to serve
under him. Antonius entered Gaul and boldly pitched his
camp next to Lepidus' army, and on 30 May Lepidus wrote
to the Senate

> my whole army, maintaining its practice of preserving the
> lives of citizens and the general peace, has mutinied, and
> to speak the truth, compelled me to take up the cause of
> the safety and preservation of so great a number of Roman
> citizens (Cicero, *Letters to his Friends* X, 35).

In other words, Lepidus had felt it safer, in view of the temper
of his troops, to combine with Antonius. Decimus Brutus,
on hearing the news, joined Plancus, proconsul of Gallia
Comata, but their combined forces were not strong enough,
even if the morale of the men had been reliable, to risk a
battle. Plancus kept writing to Octavian to march, or at least
to send some troops, but Octavian, though he said he was
coming, never came.

Although he had made it plain enough that unless he got
the consulship he would not move, the Senate was stubborn.
The leader of the opposition was Cicero, who had at first been
so forward in proposing honours, but now felt that Octavian's
demands were intolerable. Early in June Cicero wrote to

Marcus Brutus that he had crushed the intrigues for Octavian's consulship so firmly that not a senator had dared to propose it, and on 27 June he wrote again that he was still hopeful of persuading Octavian to give up his ambition. It must have been soon after that letter that Octavian sent a deputation of 400 centurions to Rome to demand the consulship for their commander. The demand was rejected, and Octavian moved his army on Rome.

The Senate at first panicked and sent out a delegation acceding to Octavian's demands. Then two African legions, which had been summoned for the war against Antonius, opportunely arrived, and it was resolved to resist with their aid and that of one legion which Pansa had left in the city. Octavian marched with a small force into the city and the three legions promptly deserted to him. The following night a rumour went round that the Martia and the fourth had rallied to the Republic and the Senate again met to organize resistance. But the rumour proved false and they hastily dispersed.

Octavian now seized the treasury and distributed to his men the donative of 2500 denarii (10,000 sesterces) which had been promised to them and never paid by the Senate. Arrangements were made for the consular elections, and he tactfully withdrew while he and his cousin Quintus Pedius were elected (19 August 43). He at length passed the *lex curiata* which made him legally Caesar's son, and his colleague passed a law setting up a special court to try Caesar's murderers. They were all condemned *in absentia*, the few who were in the city having escaped; the vote was unanimous except that one juror acquitted Marcus Brutus.

3

Triumvir

OCTAVIAN had achieved his primary objectives. He had won
the highest office in the Roman state, and had, formally
at least, avenged his father. He now immediately marched
north. Antonius had meanwhile considerably strengthened
his position. Asinius Pollio, proconsul of Further Spain, had
joined him with three legions and persuaded Munatius
Plancus to do the same. Decimus Brutus, thus isolated, had
tried to make his way to Marcus Brutus in Macedonia, but his
troops deserted, some to Antonius, some to Octavian, and
he himself was killed, on Antonius' instructions, by a Gallic
chief with whom he had taken refuge.

We do not know how long Octavian had been in communication with Antonius and Lepidus, but a meeting was now
quickly arranged. After elaborate security precautions the
three met alone on an island near Bononia, and two days of
hard bargaining followed. Antonius, Lepidus and Octavian
were to be elected by the people *tresviri reipublicae con-
stituendae* for five years (to be more precise until 31 December
38). They were to have absolute powers, and in particular to
nominate in advance all the magistrates. So far Octavian
was able to maintain parity with his senior partners. He
was however obliged to resign his hard won consulship to
Ventidius, Antonius' legate, and in the apportionment of
provinces he did badly. Antonius kept his legal provinces,
Cisalpine Gaul and Gallia Comata. Lepidus kept Gallia
Narbonensis and Hither Spain and added Further Spain. All
that was left to Octavian was Sardinia, Sicily and Africa,
militarily unimportant provinces, separated from each other
by the sea and moreover not very secure. For Sextus
Pompeius, the son of Caesar's enemy, had been appointed to
a naval command by the Senate, and had built up a powerful
fleet. The eastern provinces were not distributed, for Brutus
and Cassius had by now gained control of all Roman territory
east of the Adriatic. Next year Antonius and Octavian were

to attack them, leaving Lepidus, who would be consul, in charge of Italy and the West.

The reconciliation of Antonius and Octavian was confirmed by a marriage. Octavian had already married a daughter of Servilius Isauricus, who had been Caesar's colleague in the consulship in 48 B.C. and had since supported his son's cause in the Senate. Octavian now divorced Servilia and married Claudia, daughter of Fulvia, Antonius' wife.

The triumvirs marched on Rome, and on 27 November a tribune duly passed a plebiscite appointing them to their extraordinary office. Their first step was to proclaim a proscription; the names of 130 senators—amongst them Cicero—and a much larger number of *equites* were posted and a price put on their heads. His admirer Velleius states that Octavian resisted this savage decree, but was overborne by his colleagues; Suetonius that despite initial resistance he proved the most ruthless of the three. However that may be, the triumvirs jointly agreed that a proscription was necessary. Clemency had not paid Caesar. The Pompeians had raised revolt after revolt, and the men whom he had spared had murdered him. The triumvirs could not afford to let their enemies survive and stab them in the back while they were crushing Brutus and Cassius. Secondly, they had urgent need of money to pay the long deferred bounties they had promised to their troops.

For the second purpose the proscriptions proved disappointing. Few were willing to bid for the confiscated property of the proscribed when the political situation was so uncertain, and the prices realized were low. The triumvirs were obliged to make a levy on wealthy women, who protested boldly and got the amount reduced, and to demand from men of equestrian class a loan of five per cent of their property and a gift of a year's income.

Next year the elder Caesar was officially deified, and Octavian began to call himself 'son of the divine' instead of 'son of Gaius'. Preparations were made for the forthcoming campaign against Brutus and Cassius, but the start was delayed because Sextus Pompeius descended upon Sicily with his fleet and quickly overcame its governor, Pompeius Bithynicus. Sicily immediately became a haven for refugees from Italy and he quickly built up a substantial force. Thousands of slaves fled to him also, whom he used as rowers to man his ships. Octavian appointed Salvidienus Rufus, the young officer whose friendship he had formed at Apollonia, to undertake the campaign against Sextus, but the latter's navy proved superior. At length Antonius, who was held up at Brundisium by the superior fleet of the Republicans, insisted on Octavian's bringing his fleet to his support, and Sextus had to be left in possession of Sicily.

Brutus and Cassius had determined to stand at Philippi in Macedonia, and it was here that Antonius and Octavian defeated them in two battles on 23 October and about 14 November 42 B.C. Octavian played no part in the first action, being ill and confined to his tent, and very little in the second, when he had barely recovered: the credit for the victories went to Antonius. These battles were on a huge scale, with about twenty legions engaged on either side. They mark the effective end of the Republican party, for very many of its leaders took part, and most died fighting or, like Brutus and Cassius themselves, committed suicide. The only refugees of the Republicans were now Sextus Pompeius, just established in Sicily, and the fleet that Brutus and Cassius had raised, which still held the seas under the command of Domitius Ahenobarbus.

It was arranged that Antonius should reduce the eastern provinces to obedience and extract from them enough money to pay the troops their cash bounties. Octavian was—at his own wish—to return to Italy with a minority of the legions and all the men whose term of service had expired, and settle the latter in colonies. It was furthermore arranged that Lepidus, who was said to have opened treacherous negotiations with Sextus Pompeius, was to have his share of the provinces taken from him or at any rate reduced.

Octavian announced these arrangements on his return to Italy. He himself took over Spain from Lepidus, while Gallia Narbonensis was handed over to Antonius. Cisalpine Gaul, which was to be amalgamated with Italy, also remained for the time being under Antonius. In compensation for his losses, Octavian surrendered Africa to Lepidus, who, being in no position to resist, submitted quietly. He did not actually occupy his province until the next year.

It seems strange that so important a personage as Lepidus allowed himself to be ordered about in this unceremonious fashion by his very junior colleague. A little character sketch by Cicero (*Philippics* XIII, 4) helps to explain the anomaly:

> There is no one, members of the Senate, whose authority stands higher with me than Marcus Lepidus, both for his personal qualities and the dignity of his family . . . the Commonwealth holds Marcus Lepidus by many important ties. He has the noblest birth, every magistracy, the highest priesthood, many monuments in the city erected by himself, his brother and his ancestors; a wife of proven virtue, delightful children, an estate which is ample without being stained by the blood of fellow citizens.

In short Lepidus had all the trappings of a great noble, but under them there was only a lay figure. He lacked the ruthless qualities needed for success, or indeed survival, in these troublous times.

Octavian had no doubt chosen the task of settling the veterans because he wished thereby to win their gratitude and become their patron, and establish himself as the soldiers' friend. He had before him, however, a very invidious task, for there was no money to buy land and the estates of the proscribed had been sold for cash—which had already been spent. The only way of obtaining land was confiscation. Eighteen important cities were designated whose landowners were to be expropriated. The outcry was immense. To make matters worse, Sextus Pompeius with his fleet based on Sicily was holding up the corn ships from Africa, and Rome was threatened with starvation.

Octavian's difficulties were aggravated by the hostile attitude of one of the consuls, Lucius Antonius, brother of the triumvir, who was supported by Fulvia, Antonius' wife. Lucius protested that it was monstrous that Octavian should usurp all the credit of the settlement, and at first demanded that it should be postponed until his brother returned. Then finding that this proposal was unpopular with the troops, he demanded that the colonies for Antonius' legions should be founded by his friends. Octavian yielded this claim, Antonius' men set about brutally evicting landowners, and the odium fell on Octavian. For a time the temper of the troops turned against Octavian, and there were a number of nasty incidents; but Lucius now took up the cause of the evicted landowners, and the opinion of the troops changed. They demanded that Octavian and Lucius should settle their differences and arranged for a conference, but Lucius failed to appear, declaring that it was a trap.

Open war now followed. Octavian had sent six of his legions under Salvidienus to garrison his new province of Spain, but he still had four veteran legions in Italy and his praetorian guard. Lucius had on becoming consul raised six legions. Octavian forthwith recalled Salvidienus, but it was doubtful whether he would be able to make his way back through Gaul, which was held by Antonius' legates, Calenus, Ventidius and Pollio, and these, especially Pollio with seven legions in Cisalpine Gaul, might well intervene on Lucius' side.

Lucius, knowing that he could not face Octavian in the field with his untrained legions, marched north and threw himself into Perusia, where he expected Antonius' legates to relieve him. Octavian, assisted by Salvidienus, who had managed to make his way back to Italy, blockaded Perusia, and made his dispositions to meet Antonius' legates. Pollio and Ventidius—Calenus remained behind to hold the fort in Gallia Comata—advanced southwards, but avoided making contact with Octavian's troops. They were in an embarrassing position. Lucius was, it is true, professedly acting in his brother's interests, and had Fulvia's backing. But Octavian had throughout the quarrel maintained that he was acting in full accord with Marcus, and had produced their written agreement. Antonius might not thank his legates if they crushed his partner.

Perusia was at last starved out and surrendered at the end of February, 40 B.C. According to a much publicized legend Octavian executed 300 senators and *equites* at an altar erected to his deified father. The account given by soberer authorities is grim enough. Lucius Antonius was ostentatiously pardoned, and most of the senators and *equites* spared, but

27

Octavian executed some half dozen of his bitterest enemies, and the whole town council of Perusia with one exception— a man who had openly voted for the condemnation of Caesar's murderers.

The war ultimately proved profitable to Octavian, for Ventidius and Pollio abandoned their provinces for him to take over. By a lucky chance Calenus also died at this juncture and Octavian was able to establish his control over Gallia Comata as well. He thus ruled all the western provinces except Sicily, under Sextus Pompeius, and Africa, which Lepidus now occupied with six legions.

Octavian's most dangerous enemy was Sextus Pompeius, who continued to maintain his blockade and to harry the coasts of Italy, and now seized Sardinia. Octavian tried to reconcile him by a dynastic match, sending his diplomatic friend Maecenas to Sicily. The lady was Scribonia, an aunt of Sextus' wife. The connexion seems rather distant, and politically the match was a failure, though Scribonia presented Octavian with his only child, his daughter Julia. Sextus promptly made overtures to Antonius, whom he rightly suspected would be furious about the war of Perusia.

Antonius had since he parted from Octavian at Philippi been making a progress of Asia Minor and Syria, extracting money from the provincials and setting up and putting down kings and dynasts according to their loyalty. He was greeted at Tarsus by Cleopatra, queen of Egypt, and accepted her invitation to spend the winter at Alexandria. He apparently did not hear of the Perusian war until the spring of 40 B.C. —it must be remembered that the seas were closed to traffic from October to March—but he now at once decided to intervene in Italy, despite the fact that the Parthians were overrunning Syria; he acquired the naval aid not only of Pompeius but of the Republican admiral Ahenobarbus. He effected a landing at Brundisium, but the town resisted him. Octavian came to its support, but the fighting was soon stopped by the troops on both sides, who demanded a reconciliation between their leaders. Negotiations were conducted by Maecenas on Octavian's side and Pollio on Antonius', with Nerva to hold the balance. It was eventually agreed that the triumvirate should continue, that Italy should be shared

between all three partners, that Antonius should have all the
Greek speaking provinces from Macedonia and Cyrenaica
eastwards, Octavian all the Latin speaking provinces from
Illyricum westwards, except Africa, Lepidus' meagre share.
Antonius made Ahenobarbus proconsul of Bithynia, thus
securing his fleet for himself. Finally another dynastic match
was arranged. Fulvia had died in Greece after the Perusine
war, and Antonius now married Octavia, Octavian's sister,
whose husband Marcellus had also conveniently died.

The two triumvirs then proceeded to Rome to celebrate
the reconciliation and the marriage. Conditions were very
uncomfortable there, as Pompeius, who had been left out of
the agreement, was still pressing the blockade of Italy, and
food was very scarce and dear. Octavian was determined to
suppress Pompeius, and enacted new taxes on slaves and on
inheritances to pay for building a fleet. Riots followed, which
had to be suppressed by the troops, and eventually Octavian
agreed to Antonius' opening negotiations through Libo,
Scribonia's brother. A conference was arranged (39 B.C.) at
Misenum on one of Pompeius' ships, and it was agreed that
Pompeius should keep Sicily, Sardinia and Corsica and also
acquire the Peloponnese from Antonius. The refugees in his
dominions (except for Julius Caesar's murderers) should be
allowed to return to Italy and recover their real property or,
if proscribed, a quarter of it. In return Pompeius promised
to lift the blockade and cease from coastal raids.

It was about this time that Herod, the son of Antipater,
who had been ejected from Judaea by the Parthians in favour
of the Hasmonaean claimant Antigonus, arrived at Rome,
and was officially appointed king of Judaea and adjacent
territories by the Senate. Antonius at last turned his attention
to the Parthians, who had by now not only overrun all Syria
and Palestine, but most of Asia Minor, led by the 'Parthicus
imperator' Labienus, Julius Caesar's legate who had deserted
to Pompeius Magnus. Even now Antonius did not go himself,
but sent Ventidius, one of the new men of the triumviral
period who had started life as a muleteer. At this period one
of Octavian's brilliant new men, Salvidienus, who had been
with him at Apollonia in 43 B.C. and was now governor
of Gaul, met his end. Antonius, with his usual frankness,

AUGUSTUS

revealed to Octavian that Salvidienus had made treacherous
approaches to him at the time of the siege of Brundisium.
Octavian recalled him from Gaul and had him condemned
by the Senate for treason.

The peace with Sextus Pompeius did not last long. Pompeius was aggrieved because Antonius would not cede the
Peloponnese to him until he had paid or given a bond for the
arrears which the cities owed to him. This was at any rate
the ostensible reason for his reviving the blockade of Italy,
though some said that, under the influence of his freedman
Menodorus, who had always been against the peace, he was
dissatisfied with his inferior position in relation to the triumvirs. It so happened that Octavian at the same time contributed to the breach, divorcing the elderly Scribonia, being,
as he later wrote, 'weary of the perversity of her character'.
His motive was not to make a break with Pompeius, but
to marry Livia, the young and beautiful wife of Tiberius
Claudius Nero. Livia came of one of the most aristocratic
families of Rome, but it was a love match, and Octavian was
in such a hurry that he got the special approval of the
pontifices to marry her while pregnant by her first husband.
Nero raised no objection, and actually betrothed his wife to
Octavian.

The war opened well (38 B.C.) with the desertion of
Pompeius' freedman, Menodorus, who was governor of Sardinia and Corsica, and brought over the islands with a fleet
and army. But subsequent operations against Sicily were
disastrous. Lepidus and Antonius were asked to assist, but
Lepidus took no notice, and Antonius having arrived at
Brundisium and not found Octavian awaiting him, sailed
back, sending him a letter reproaching him for breaking
the treaty. Next year (37 B.C.) was devoted to building a new
and more powerful fleet. Ships were constructed and extra
taxes levied for the purpose, slaves were requisitioned to
be rowers, and, so that the crews could practise in safety,
a large inland harbour was constructed by connecting Lake
Avernus with the Lucrine Lake and the Lucrine Lake with
the sea. The man in charge of the construction and training programme was Octavian's old and trusty friend
Agrippa. Maecenas, though he held no magistracy and
30

was still only an equestrian, was given charge of Rome and Italy.

Octavian again asked Antonius' aid and this time he brought it, sailing with 120 ships to Tarentum. Now that his preparations were so far advanced, Octavian seems to have been somewhat ungracious about this generous, if tardy, aid, which involved him in the obligation to furnish Antonius with 20,000 legionaries for the Parthian war—an obligation which he never honoured. Octavia, however, smoothed over the ill feeling. Lepidus was also induced to join in the attack on Sicily in substantial force, perhaps by Antonius' persuasion. Finally the powers of the triumvirate, which had inadvertently been allowed to expire on 31 December 38, were extended five years to 31 December 33.

Next year (36 B.C.) a triple attack was launched on Sicily by Octavian himself, Agrippa and Lepidus. Octavian was, as usual, dismally unsuccessful, but the others effected landings, and a final great naval battle was won at Naulochus. Sextus Pompeius sailed off with the remnants of his fleet to the East, where he was later defeated and killed by Antonius' generals. Lepidus tried to take Sicily for himself, but his troops mutinied, and Octavian was able to take them over, with the Pompeians, and depose Lepidus. His life was spared, but he lived under guard henceforth. Statilius Taurus was sent to take over Africa.

Octavian's troubles were not over. His own men clamoured for discharge and their long promised land and bounties. Octavian had to compromise, discharging those who had fought at Mutina or Philippi, some 20,000 men, and giving the rest a bonus of 500 denarii each. The money he secured by a levy of 1600 talents on the Sicilian cities, which were treated as rebels for having fallen under Pompeius' dominion. The veterans he planted partly at Capua, where there was land to spare from the earlier settlement, partly at Tauromenium and perhaps other Sicilian cities, whose citizens were driven out. He also degraded the political status of the Sicilian cities. They had been given Latin status by Julius Caesar, and the Roman citizenship by Antonius. In the official register reproduced by Pliny, Messina is a *municipium,* there are five colonies and three Latin cities and all the rest are reduced to stipendiary status. This war is described in the *Res Gestae* (25) as follows:

> I pacified the sea from pirates. In that war I captured and returned to their owners for punishment about 30,000 slaves who had fled from their owners and taken up arms against the Republic.

He does not mention that he crucified the 6000 slaves whose owners could not be traced.

Honours were heaped upon Octavian on his return to Rome. Rather more than an honour was the vote of tribunician sacrosanctity, which not only did something for his personal security, but stressed the tie with his adoptive father and his support of the *populares*. He was also offered the office of *pontifex maximus*, which his adoptive father had held, and to which he felt that he had an hereditary claim, but in deference to the law that the office was for life, he refused it so long as Lepidus lived. In return for these honours he abolished some taxes and remitted arrears, and promised to restore their functions to the Republican magistrates. These had become a mockery under the triumvirs. Their numbers had been greatly increased by Caesar, which shocked conservatives. But latterly the magistrates had been holding office for a few weeks only to be rapidly replaced by suffects: in 38 B.C. there had been sixty-seven praetors (instead of the republican eight, and Caesar's sixteen). They naturally did nothing. The posts were valued solely as giving access to and precedence in the Senate, and the social prestige resulting therefrom. Finally Octavian promised that he would restore the Republic as soon as Antonius returned from the Parthian wars. These gestures were evidently intended to please the senatorial and equestrian orders. Many refugees had now returned from Sicily and elsewhere. It was obviously politic to try to gain their goodwill in case a clash with Antonius should come, and no doubt Octavian intended that it should come; he had a right to the whole empire as his father's heir.

From the time of the Sicilian war Octavian adopted a new name. He had hitherto, since his adoption and his adoptive father's deification, been Gaius Iulius *divi filius* Caesar. He now dropped *praenomen* and *nomen,* and took a new *praenomen*, Imperator, thus becoming Imperator Caesar *divi filius*. It seems probable that he resuscitated the cognomen Imperator which the Senate had voted to Julius Caesar but he had never used, and following a prevalent fashion used his father's cognomen as a *praenomen*—one of Gnaeus Pompeius Magnus' sons called himself Magnus Pompeius. Imperator is regarded as a title by Dio, but it was not so originally and had no constitutional significance, though it carried an aura of military authority. It is not clear why Octavian henceforth dropped the ancient and honourable name of Julius.

In 35 and 34 B.C. Octavian conducted two campaigns in Illyricum. His main object was no doubt to keep his troops busy and in good training, and to win for himself the military prestige which sadly he lacked. But the result was useful. Hitherto Illyricum had consisted of little but the coast road, which was constantly threatened or interrupted by the war-like tribes of the mountainous interior. Octavian conquered the hill country, penetrating as far as Siscia and the Save, and thus for the first time created a secure overland route from Italy to Macedonia and the East.

Agrippa, having played the major part in the reduction of Sextus Pompeius and been rewarded with the consulship in 37 B.C., now won popularity for Octavian in a more modest sphere. In 34 B.C. he took the inferior office of aedile and thoroughly overhauled the aqueduct system of Rome, which had become very dilapidated, compiled a register of those entitled to draw a private supply, and supplied a gang of slaves, about 250 strong, to carry out inspections and routine maintenance.

When he left Italy after his marriage Antonius spent the better part of the next three years (39–37 B.C.) at Athens with Octavia, while his generals Ventidius and Sosius beat the Parthians out of Asia Minor and Syria. It was not until 37 B.C. that Herod was finally installed in the kingdom voted to him by the Senate in 40 B.C. When Antonius next visited Italy for the conference of Tarentum in 37 B.C. he sent Octavia back to Rome from Corcyra, alleging that she could not accompany him on the Parthian campaign which he planned for next year. Having arrived in Syria he summoned

Cleopatra from Egypt, though she was not to play any part in the expedition, and mustered his troops, of which there are said to have been 60,000 Roman infantry, 10,000 Spanish and Gallic cavalry, and vast numbers of allied forces, including 6000 horse and 7000 foot from Artavasdes, king of Armenia. He also made some important territorial dispositions, appointing Archelaus, the grandson of Mithradates VI's Greek general of that name, king of Cappadocia, Amyntas, the Greek secretary of the Galatian king Deiotarus, king of Galatia, Lycaonia and Pamphylia (he already held Pisidia), and Polemo, son of Zeno, a distinguished rhetorician of Laodicea, as king of Pontus, to which he added Armenia Minor in 34 B.C. These appointments were a rather daring innovation. The Roman government had hitherto confirmed native kings in their dominions, and sometimes enlarged them, or appointed new kings from the existing royal families. But it was a new thing to promote able commoners, and to give them what had hitherto been provincial territory. It was, however, successful policy. Antonius' nominees were men of marked ability—and Octavian acknowledged the fact by confirming most of them—while the areas they ruled were unsuitable for direct rule by a Roman governor, since they needed closer supervision and control than could be given to them by annual proconsuls.

Antonius' other territorial dispositions were more questionable. He granted to Cleopatra, with her children by him, the twins Alexander Helios and Cleopatra Selene (born in 40 B.C.), whom he formally acknowledged as his, Cyrenaica, Cyprus, parts of Crete, Cilicia Tracheia, the Ituraean principality, the Syrian coast as far north as the Eleutherus (except for the free cities of Tyre and Sidon), the district of Jericho (out of Herod's kingdom), and a part of the Nabataean kingdom. This was practically the old Ptolemaic Empire at its greatest extent; Herod's kingdom, which Cleopatra asked for, would have completed it, but at this point Antonius was firm. There was no pretence of the administrative or military needs of the Roman Empire; it was sheer favouritism.

In the spring of 36 B.C. Antonius launched his great Parthian expedition. The plan, a wise one, was to avoid the Mesopotamian steppe and desert, which was, as Crassus had learned to his cost in 53 B.C., ideal for Parthian cavalry tactics, and to march through southern Armenia into Media. Antonius successfully reached Media and besieged its capital Phraaspa. He failed to take it, and after wasting months on the siege did not start back until winter was approaching. His difficulties were increased by the desertion of the king of Armenia. He displayed all his best qualities in the terrible retreat, but lost about a quarter of his men, partly from enemy action, but mostly from exhaustion, exposure and disease. Having reached Phoenicia he sent a message to Cleopatra to bring money and clothing to succour the army. But when next spring Octavia arrived in Greece with more clothing and baggage animals, and 10,000 picked men to serve as his praetorian guard, Antonius sent her a letter refusing the gifts and ordering her to return to Italy.

In this year (35 B.C.) he undertook no military operations. In 34 B.C. he marched into Armenia, and having lured king Artavasdes into his camp took him prisoner and annexed his kingdom. This exploit was celebrated by an extraordinary triumph at Alexandria in the course of which Cleopatra and her son by Julius Caesar, Ptolemy Caesar, commonly called Caesarion (little Caesar), then aged thirteen, were proclaimed Queen and King of Kings, and allotted Egypt and Cyprus. Alexander Helios was made king of Armenia, and of Media and the rest of the Parthian Empire when it should be conquered; Philadelphus (born 36 B.C.) received Phoenicia, Syria and Cilicia; Cleopatra Selene had to be content with Cyrenaica.

War between Octavian and Antonius was now obviously inevitable. Antonius had inflicted a personal slight on Octavia, Octavian's sister, by sending her home and openly acknowledging Cleopatra as his wife—it was not of course a legal Roman marriage, since a Roman citizen could not marry a foreigner, but a marriage none the less. He had moreover shown complete lack of responsibility in bestowing upon her and her family all the Roman territory beyond the Taurus. Worst of all, by recognizing Ptolemy Caesar he had thrown doubts on Octavian's claim to be the one and only son and heir of the dictator. A propaganda war began in which each party hurled reproaches of bad faith at the other, and, in the normal Roman manner, accusations of every vice. So far the contest was tolerably even. But Octavian held a trump card. He could exploit Roman xenophobia against the sinister Egyptian queen, whose most solemn oath, it was alleged, was 'as I shall deliver judgment on the Capitol', and could pour contempt on Antonius as her helpless slave, which he had proved himself to be by his fantastic donations.

It is difficult to judge how far this propaganda was success-ful. A good test is the picture of the battle of Actium on Aeneas' shield as drawn by Virgil in the *Aeneid* (VIII, 678–700):

> On the one side was Augustus Caesar leading the Italians to battle, with the Fathers and the people, the Penates and the great gods, erect on the lofty poop. . . . On the other Antonius, with barbaric wealth and various arms, victorious from the peoples of the dawn and the Red Sea's shore, brings with him Egypt and the might of the East and furthest Bactria. He is followed, shame upon it, by his Egyptian wife . . . the queen in the midst summons her troops with her native sistrum, and turns no more to see the double snakes behind her. All kinds of monstrous gods and the barking Anubis turn their weapons against Neptune and Venus and Minerva.

It is difficult to believe that Virgil wrote this with his tongue in his cheek, as a deliberate piece of propaganda. Nor was it official policy by the time that he wrote the eighth book of the *Aeneid* to blacken the characters of Antonius or Cleopatra; both are studiously ignored in the *Res Gestae* together with the whole of the civil wars. The picture must then represent Virgil's own feelings, and since Virgil was a typical patriotic but non-political Italian, it would suggest that the ordinary public mostly accepted the orientalized Antonius and his sinister Egyptian queen.

It is even more difficult to discover what Antonius was about during the ten years that he spent in the East. Though capable of great feats of endurance in crises, such as the retreats from Mutina and from Parthia, he seems to have been idle by temperament, and spent long periods at Athens with Octavia and at Alexandria with Cleopatra, when there were urgent tasks to be done. His great problem was the Parthian menace, which he bungled badly. The disastrous failure of the expedition of 36 B.C. was not, it is true, entirely his fault, but the desultory operations in Armenia in 34–33 did nothing to retrieve the situation. In his last years he clearly fell completely under the spell of Cleopatra. Nothing else can explain the territorial grants of 36, the still more fantastic donations of Alexandria in 34, and his insistence, despite the urgent pleas of his Roman friends, on taking Cleopatra with him to Actium. It has been urged that only so could he obtain the use of the Egyptian fleet and money and supplies for his own forces; but it is ridiculous to suggest that he could not have ordered Cleopatra as an allied queen to put at his disposal whatever he wanted, if he had chosen to assert himself.

Cleopatra's aims are clearer. They were dynastic, to restore the kingdom of the Ptolemies to its ancient greatness. Her only weapons were her beauty and charm, but with them she had virtually achieved her ends by 36 B.C. She seems then to have indulged in megalomaniac dreams of a great eastern empire, but it is most unlikely that she ever intended to rule in Rome. She would have needed to go to Rome and indeed live there, as she had done after her affair with Caesar, to maintain her influence over Antonius, but she must have realized that Antonius would rule the West.

Meanwhile Octavian made constitutional preparations. His triumviral powers would expire on 31 December 33 B.C., and he had no intention of getting them renewed. It would stultify his promises of restoring the Republic, and moreover Antonius' powers would have to be renewed simultaneously, or he would incur the odium of bad faith to his partner. Nor could he become consul, for the consulships had long been arranged beforehand by mutual consent between him and Antonius, and once again he would incur odium by breach of the agreement. Unfortunately the two consuls of 32 would both be Antonius' friends, Domitius Ahenobarbus and Gaius Sosius.

Octavian's solution of this problem was revealed when the inhabitants of Italy rallied city by city and spontaneously swore an oath of loyalty to him, and the provincials of Gaul, Spain, Africa, Sicily and Sardinia followed suit. We do not

know the exact wording of this oath, but we do possess the
text of the oath taken by the Paphlagonians thirty years later
when they became Roman subjects on the death of their king
(Ehrenberg and Jones, *Documents* 315). It runs as follows:

> I swear by Jupiter, Juno and all the gods and goddesses,
> that I will be loyal to Caesar and his children and descend-
> ants all the time of my life by word and deed and thought,
> holding as friends whomsoever they so hold, and consider-
> ing as enemies whomsoever they so judge, and for their
> interests I will spare neither body nor soul nor life nor
> children, but will endure every peril for their cause. If I see
> or hear anything being said or planned or done against
> them, I will lay information and I will be the enemy of such
> sayer or planner or doer; whoever they themselves judge to
> be their enemies, them I will pursue and resist by land and
> by sea with arms and with iron. If I do anything contrary to
> this oath or not according as I have sworn, I invoke death
> and destruction upon myself and my body and soul and
> children and all my race and interests to the last generation
> of my children's children, and may not the earth nor the sea
> receive the bodies of my family and my descendants, nor
> bear crops for them.

It may be noted that the oath is not a public declaration of
allegiance to the head of the state, but an affirmation of
loyalty to Octavian and his descendants personally, and a
pledge to support him against his private enemies—the Greek
word is different for a public enemy of the state. In accordance with the personal character of the oath Octavian excused
the people of Bononia from taking it, since they were hereditary clients of the Antonii. He claims in the *Res Gestae* that
by this oath the Roman people demanded him as leader in
the forthcoming war, and that he thereby acquired universal
power. Constitutionalists may not have agreed.

On 1 January 32 the consuls summoned the Senate, and
Sosius made a speech in favour of Antonius and violently
denounced Octavian but the motion which he proposed
against Octavian was vetoed by a tribune. Octavian, who
had deliberately absented himself from the meeting, demanded that the consuls publish Antonius' latest des-

patches, which he knew announced the conquest of Armenia, but also the donations to Cleopatra and her children. The consuls, well aware that the odium of the donations would outweigh the credit of Armenia, refused. Octavian now, in virtue of the powers he claimed from the oath, summoned the Senate, and entering with an escort of soldiers and armed civilian supporters, took his seat between the consuls and made a speech justifying himself; no one ventured to reply. Having been thus flouted, the consuls thought it best to flee to Antonius, and were followed by a number of senators. Octavian replaced the consuls with a pair of more compliant nobles. Antonius next sent a formal divorce to Octavia, and Octavian, having learned that Antonius' will was deposited with the Vestal Virgins, demanded it from them, and, being refused, took it, and read it to the Senate. It contained an affirmation that Ptolemy Caesar was a true son of the dictator, extravagant legacies to Antonius' children by Cleopatra, and instructions that even if he died at Rome his corpse should be sent to Cleopatra at Alexandria. There was some feeling in the Senate that it was in bad taste to publish a man's will when he was alive, but with the general public this feeling was overpowered by the horror inspired by the will's contents, particularly the last clause. Then at length war was solemnly declared on Cleopatra, and Antonius was deprived of the consulship for which he was designated the next year.

Military, naval and financial preparations now began for the war. Antonius mustered his forces at Ephesus. He had altogether thirty legions, but used only about two-thirds of them for the war, keeping the rest as garrisons in Cyrenaica and Syria. He also had substantial contingents from his numerous client kings. His fleet is said by Plutarch to have numbered 500, of which Cleopatra contributed 60. Octavian mustered his forces, which seem to have been rather smaller, in the southern ports of Italy. He tried also to impose war taxes—on freeborn citizens a quarter of their rents, on freedmen owning over 50,000 denarii an eighth of their property. Despite the recent oath, there were riots and incendiarism.

On 1 January Octavian became consul for the third time, his colleague being Valerius Messala Corvinus, who was not only a nobleman, but had been proscribed, had fought under Cassius at Philippi, and had joined Antonius: he had later left Antonius for Octavian, and fought in the Sicilian war against Sextus Pompeius and in Illyricum. He now joined Octavian in the war against Antonius, together with more than seven hundred senators; when the aged and unfit are eliminated, there cannot have been many members of the Senate—which at this time numbered over a thousand—with Antonius. Maecenas was again, as in the Sicilian war, put in charge of Rome and Italy during Octavian's absence.

Antonius moved his forces up to the Epirot and Greek coast from Corcyra to Methone, where they were largely dependent on sea-borne supplies from Egypt. Neither side was very anxious to take the risk of an opposed landing, but Octavian no doubt realized how disastrous it would be to his prestige and popularity to allow the sacred soil of Italy to be ravaged by an invader, and Antonius, dominated though he was by Cleopatra—he had several times rejected strong representations by his Roman friends that he must leave her behind for this campaign—may have realized that the arrival of Cleopatra as a conqueror in Italy would confirm all Octavian's propaganda and arouse passionate resistance. So Octavian and Agrippa crossed the Adriatic with their respective squadrons from Brundisium and Tarentum. Agrippa seized Methone in the extreme south. Octavian sailed northwards and effected an unopposed landing on the coast of Epirus, whence he marched south and seized and fortified the promontory which closes the gulf of Ambracia on the north. Antonius concentrated his forces on Actium, the opposite promontory, and there followed a long period of desultory fighting, while Agrippa by a series of brilliant raids captured two more valuable ports, Leucas and Patrae. The sea being closed to him, Antonius was reduced to carrying up his supplies by trains of porters, pressing respectable citizens of Greek cities, including Plutarch's great grandfather Nicarchus, into this service.

The result was that Antonius' men were weakened by hunger. They also suffered from malaria, being camped in a marshy area, whereas Octavian had occupied the only high ground. Morale fell and there were frequent desertions, both by high ranking Romans, and by several client kings, including Antonius's recent appointment Amyntas. Antonius and Cleopatra decided that they must somehow break the blockade before it was too late, but their plan remains an unsolved mystery. It seems likely that they intended to break out with the fleet, carrying as many legionaries as possible, and sail to Egypt, while the rest of the army were to march overland eastward through Macedonia and Thrace. In favour of this version is the fact that they burned all the ships they could not man with rowers, and that the ships were ordered to take their sails, which they normally did not carry in battle. The plan was not however revealed to the captains, or to the land army, presumably for fear of weakening their morale; the sails were said to be for pursuing the defeated enemy. Whatever the plan was, it miscarried. On the day of the battle (2 September 31 B.C.) Cleopatra got away with the Egyptian squadron and Antonius followed with a few ships, but the bulk of the fleet either failed to receive the order or was too heavily engaged, and was left behind to be destroyed or captured by Octavian; he says that he took 300 triremes and larger warships. The land army also failed to move. Canidius, its commander, fled to Antonius, and the men surrendered on terms to Octavian after a week.

Antonius landed in Cyrenaica hoping to rally the five legions he had there, but they refused to obey him and he went on to Egypt. Cleopatra sailed straight to Alexandria and made sure of her position by executing her potential enemies and confiscating their property. When the news from Actium came through it became obvious that all they could do was to hold out in Egypt, and they had little serious hope of doing that. Octavian meanwhile, having founded a City of Victory, Nicopolis, on the site of his camp, and endowed it with a huge territory, including the ancient but decayed cities of Ambracia and Anactorium and the whole of Aetolia, and founded quadrennial Actian games, moved through Macedonia and Greece and then crossed to Samos and Rhodes, rewarding and punishing cities and kings and dynasts according to which side they had taken. The principal kings were all confirmed. Amyntas, who had already deserted before

41

Actium, had Cilicia Tracheia, which Antonius had ceded to Cleopatra, added to his kingdom of Galatia. Archelaus and Polemo were confirmed in Cappadocia and Pontus; the latter lost Armenia Minor to an exiled king of Media. Herod, who had on Antonius' orders stayed at home to chastise Malchus, king of Arabia, sailed to Rhodes, having first killed the aged Hyrcanus, the Hasmonaean claimant to the throne, and by an adroit speech, in which he boasted of his devoted loyalty to Antonius and promised the same to Octavian, got his kingdom confirmed and enlarged by half a dozen Greek cities.

Octavian returned to Athens, where he was initiated in the mysteries of Eleusis, and had entered upon his fourth consulship, with Licinius Crassus (30 B.C.), when he received an urgent message from Maecenas in Italy. Maecenas had detected and suppressed a conspiracy by Lepidus, the son of the deposed triumvir. More serious was a military mutiny. Octavian had after Actium discharged all the men, both in his own and in Antonius' army, who had served over a long period, and sent them under Agrippa's command to Italy, with orders to disperse them in small groups. This precaution had not proved adequate and they were clamouring for their bounties. Octavian took the risk of crossing to Italy in mid winter—and actually incurred some serious hazards—and managed to quiet the veterans, by giving some of them part payment of their bounties, the money for which he had collected from the indemnities he had been levying in Greece and Macedonia and Asia, and settling others in Italian towns, compensating the expelled landowners with land in Dyrrachium and Philippi, which he had presumably confiscated from their pro-Antonian citizens.

This done, he made the perilous return journey, and advancing through Syria captured Pelusium and moved on Alexandria. Antonius and Cleopatra made no serious resistance, and had in fact been negotiating for some time. Octavian's objective was to capture Cleopatra alive to display in his triumph and to secure Antonius' death without being responsible for it. He failed in the first aim, but succeeded in the second, for both Antonius and Cleopatra committed suicide. He killed Ptolemy Caesar, who was an obvious threat to his own position, and Antullus, Antonius' eldest son. His other children he spared and sent to Rome, where they were brought up by Octavia. Nothing more is heard of the two boys, but Cleopatra Selene was in due course married to Juba, the learned king of Mauretania.

4

The Restoration of the Republic

OCTAVIAN forthwith annexed the kingdom of Egypt, making it a province of the Roman people; the anomalous administrative system which he established now and which lasted for three centuries will be described in Chapter 8. In the autumn he marched north again through Syria and Asia Minor to Samos, where he entered upon his fifth consulship with his nephew Sextus Appuleius, son of his half sister Octavia Major, as his colleague (29 B.C.). At Rome meanwhile the Senate and people had been voting him innumerable honours—triumphal arches, crowns, games, supplications and so forth —which not even Cassius Dio could bring himself to enumerate in full—and some more interesting powers, a tribunician right of *auxilium* which extended not only within the *pomerium* and the first milestone but, it would seem, throughout the Empire; the right to judge cases upon appeal; and a 'vote of Minerva', that is a power of pardon, in criminal cases heard by the *iudicia publica*. He also received the power to create patricians by a *lex Saenia*. The honour which pleased him most was the closing of the Temple of Janus by decree of the Senate. The temple was closed only when Rome was at peace with all the world, and it had only been closed twice before in history. There were, it is true, two wars in progress, one against the Treveri and sundry German tribes in Gaul, and another against the Cantabri and the Astures in Spain. But the end of the civil war overshadowed these minor conflicts.

At length he returned to Italy and nearly two years after the battle of Actium celebrated from 13 August 29 B.C. onwards a triple triumph for the conquest of Illyricum, the battle of Actium, and the annexation of Egypt. He had in the previous year settled the claims of his soldiers and veterans, for he now had ample funds drawn from the accumulated treasure of Egypt, so ample that he was able to refuse the gold crowns offered by the cities of Italy. The details are uncertain, as in the *Res Gestae* he combines this settlement with the next great settlement in 14 B.C. On this occasion he settled 120,000 veterans in colonies, and gave them each a triumphal donative of 1000 sesterces. Altogether on the two occasions he paid out 600 millions for Italian land and 280 millions for provincial land. He boasts to have been first to pay cash for the land required. Altogether he founded twenty-eight colonies in Italy and many more in various provinces, Africa, Sicily, Macedonia, both Spains, Achaea, Asia, Syria, Gallia Narbonensis and Pisidia.

It was time for Octavian to take steps towards fulfilling his promise to restore the Republic when the civil wars were over. He had been consul every year since Actium, and claimed universal power through the oath of 33 B.C. This was symbolized by the fact that all 24 lictors walked before him, and his colleague had none. On 1 January 28, when he entered on his sixth consulate with Agrippa for the second time, he gave up this invidious distinction, sharing the lictors with his colleague in the usual way. He then obtained censorial powers for himself and Agrippa and conducted a census, in which 4,063,000 citizens were registered, and conducted a revision of the roll of the Senate. This was the real object of the whole operation, for in any restored Republic the Senate must hold a key position, and it must therefore be a body which commanded respect. There is no hint that this was a political purge: no Republican or Antonian is known to have been expelled, and a good many are known to have been prominent in the Senate later. They were, after all, so reduced in numbers as to be no longer dangerous, and their tacit acceptance of the new regime would give it respectability. What Octavian wished to get rid of were the large numbers of obscure and sometimes disreputable characters who had got in by interest in the triumviral period. The Senate now numbered over a thousand, and he wished to bring it down to the Sullan figure of six hundred. He did not succeed, but fifty were persuaded to resign and allowed to keep the externals of senatorial rank, while 150 were expelled. He used his powers under the *lex Saenia* to create some new patricians.

Next year (27 B.C.) he was consul for the seventh time with

Agrippa again as his colleague. On 1 January, to quote his own words (*Res Gestae* 34)

> After I had extinguished the civil wars, being by universal consent in possession of everything, I transferred the commonwealth from my own power to the free choice of the Roman Senate and people.

The Senate, no doubt led by the minority who were in the know, loudly protested against his thus deserting the Republic, and a motion was apparently carried conferring upon him an ill-defined guardianship over the state—

> that he may have the right and power to do and perform whatsoever he shall judge to be in the interest of the commonwealth or the majesty of things divine and human, public and private (Ehrenberg and Jones, *Documents* 364).

Octavian objected that the responsibility was too great, and it was eventually agreed that he should receive as his consular province for ten years the unsettled parts of the Empire which required military defence. These were defined as Spain, except for the civilized area in the south henceforth known as Baetica; Gaul, including Narbonensis; Syria, including Cilicia and Cyprus; and Egypt. In order to manage this large and scattered area he received the right, like Pompey and the other holders of special commands, to appoint numerous legates of consular and praetorian rank. He also, like Pompey under the *lex Manilia,* was given the right to declare war and make treaties. This incidentally, as Strabo says, gave him the control of all kings and dynasts, who were technically foreign powers. He also commanded a very large part of the army. It must be remembered however that among the 'public provinces' which were administered by other proconsuls, were Africa, which always kept one legion, and Illyricum and Macedonia, which were still at this date exposed frontier provinces and must have had several legions each. Finally, as a recognition of his restoration of the Republic Octavian was awarded the cognomen of Augustus, by which he was henceforth called. It is said that he would have liked to be called Romulus, the second founder of Rome, but was warned that this had too regal a connotation. 'Augustus', had a vague religious flavour, which suggested that he was more than human. The result of these arrangements is thus lyrically described by Velleius Paterculus (II, 89):

> When Caesar returned to Italy and the city, the concourse and applause whereby he was greeted by all men, ages, and ranks, and the magnificence of his triumphs and his games could not be worthily expressed in a regular historical work, much less in this brief summary. Thereafter men could hope for nothing from the gods, the gods could give nothing to men, nothing could be the object of prayer and the gift of good fortune, which Augustus did not bestow upon the Republic and upon the world after his return to the city. After twenty years the civil wars were ended, foreign wars buried, peace recalled, the fury of arms everywhere lulled to sleep; their force was restored to the laws, authority to the courts, its majesty to the Senate; the rule of the magistrates was restored to its old form—only two praetors were added to the eight. The ancient original form of the commonwealth was recalled. Tillage returned to the fields, its honour to religion, security to men, firm possession of his property to the individual.

As Velleius says, the ancient form of the Republic was restored, as it existed before Caesar's dictatorship; only his two additional *aediles Cereales* were preserved. The quaestors were reduced from forty to the Sullan figure of twenty, the praetors from sixteen to the Sullan eight—Velleius is wrong on this point: the praetors were not raised to ten until 23 B.C. There were two consuls only, and no suffects were permitted. All these magistrates were once more elected, and there is no reason to believe that the elections were not free. Indeed Augustus was obliged in 18 B.C. to tighten the law on electoral corruption. Augustus, of course, like all other great men, canvassed for candidates whom he favoured, and, as he was a very great man, his support was generally efficacious. But the evidence suggests that he did not abuse his influence, backing only a small number of favourites for each office; in particular, he seems to have refrained from interfering in the consular elections.

All these officers performed their traditional functions,

though as time went on the aediles lost most of theirs. Praetors and consuls, after an interval of five years, as enacted by Pompeius' law, drew lots for provinces. Africa and Asia came to be regarded as the consular provinces, the praetors (who like the consuls took the title of proconsul) drew between Baetica, Sicily, Sardinia and Corsica, Illyricum, Macedonia, Achaea, Crete and Cyrene, Bithynia and Pontus.

During his seventh consulate Augustus undertook the repair of the Via Flaminia as far as Ariminum, rebuilding all the bridges except two; it was evidentally in a bad way. He paid for this out of his own pocket, and he induced others who had celebrated triumphs—and held large sums in booty (*manubiae*)—to do the same for the other principal roads.

In the same year Marcus Crassus, proconsul of Macedonia, received a triumph for his military successes in Thrace. He also claimed the *spolia opima,* an antique honour only awarded twice before in the history of Rome, for having killed an enemy chief with his own hand. Augustus was apparently jealous of this distinction; a monopoly of military glory was essential to his position. Accordingly he opportunely discovered an ancient linen corslet on which Cossus, the first holder of the *spolia opima,* was described as consul; the tradition was that he was a military tribune. On the strength of this find Augustus ruled that only a consul was entitled to the prize.

When the consular elections came on, Augustus stood, and was naturally elected, his colleague being Statilius Taurus, a military man of Lucanian origin, who had served Augustus well in the Sicilian war and at Actium. We are not told what the reaction to Augustus' candidature was. The normal Republican custom was that when a consul was allotted his province he went off and governed it as proconsul. Pompeius, it is true, had after his consulship in 55 B.C. hung about near Rome for two years, governing his provinces through legates, and had not given up his provinces even when he was created consul in 52 B.C.: but this was hardly a good precedent. Republicans may before the end of 27 B.C. have begun to have doubts about Augustus' restoration of the Republic.

After his election Augustus proceeded in the autumn to his province of Gaul, where he held a census. This was the first of his many provincial censuses, on which he based a new and more equitable system of taxation (see Chapter 10). He went on to Spain, where he entered on his eighth consulship at Tarraco, and conducted a strenuous campaign against the Astures and Cantabri. This was continued into the next year, when Augustus was again consul (for the ninth time, with Marcus Junius Silanus, a noble who had joined Sextus Pompeius and then Antonius, but deserted the latter at Actium). He fell ill, and had to retire to Tarraco, but his lieutenants carried on, and appeared to have reduced the tribes, so much so that the Senate again voted that the Temple of Janus be closed. This was premature, for the Spaniards rebelled once more in the next year (24 B.C.) and again in 22 and 19 and 16. A large veteran colony called Emerita Augusta was established at this time in the territory of the Lusitanians.

In other parts of the Empire meanwhile Terentius Varro Murena ruthlessly subdued the troublesome Alpine tribe of the Salassi, selling 36,000 men into slavery, and founding in their territory the veteran colony of Augusta Praetoria, formed from veterans of the praetorian guard. In 25 B.C. King Amyntas was killed fighting another unruly tribe, the Homonadenses. His kingdom was annexed, except for Cilicia Trachia, which was granted to Archelaus of Cappadocia, and added to Augustus' provinces under the style of Galatia; a colony was founded at Caesarea Antioch, the principal town of his kingdom. Juba, the learned king of Numidia, to whom Augustus had married Antonius' daughter Cleopatra Selene, was transferred from his own kingdom of Numidia, which was annexed to Africa, to Mauretania, a much larger but less developed and less civilized region. He was obliged to accept a large number of veteran colonies in his coastal towns.

Cornelius Gallus, the prefect of Egypt whom Augustus had appointed in 30 B.C., subdued a rebellion in the Thebaid and made a treaty with the Ethiopians, whereby the Romans appointed a native paramount chief to rule the Triacontaschoenus, the stretch of the Nile between the First and Second Cataracts. He then began to carve on the temples absurdly grandiose incriptions in Pharhaonic phraseology. Augustus recalled him and banned him from all his provinces. The Senate forthwith voted that he should be tried in the court of *maiestas* and exiled and his property confiscated. Gallus committed suicide. Augustus, who was away in Spain when all this happened, expressed gratitude to the Senate for their prompt loyalty, but lamented his own fate, that he alone was not allowed to quarrel with his friends as much as he wanted. This remark was not necessarily hypocritical; a man of Gallus' stature was no threat to his power, and he appears to have been merely foolishly romantic.

After this, Augustus tells us in the *Res Gestae* (26):

> On my orders and under my auspices two armies were led at about the same time into Ethiopia and into Arabia called the Fortunate, and large forces of the enemy of both peoples were killed in battle and several towns captured. In Ethiopia the army reached the town of Nabata, which is very close to Meroe, in Arabia it advanced as far as the territory of the Sabaeans to the town of Mariba.

Augustus suggests that the expeditions were made merely to show the flag in the remotest parts of Asia and Africa, and that they were both equally successful. Even so he exaggerates a little. Meroe was 200 miles upstream from Nabata, and Mariba was not, as Augustus' readers were no doubt meant to assume, the Sabaean capital Mariaba, but a very insignificant town some way north of it.

We have a full account of both expeditions from Strabo, who was a personal friend of Aelius Gallus, Cornelius Gallus' successor as prefect of Egypt, who commanded the forces destined for Arabia. Arabia Felix was a land of legendary wealth, and its people were believed to possess vast stocks of gold and silver. For they sold the incense and other aromatic plants which grew in their country, and also the precious stones which were believed to be found there but actually came from India, for very high prices in cash to Roman merchants, and never bought anything in return. Gallus' instructions were to win them over by persuasion, or if that failed to subdue them by force. In either case Augustus expected to get access to their accumulated wealth.

In 25 B.C. Gallus assembled an army of 10,000 men, mostly Roman troops but including a contingent of 500 men from Herod, King of Judaea, and another of 1000 from Obodas,

King of Nabataean Arabia. These last were commanded by Syllaeus, the all-powerful vizier of King Obodas, who was to serve as guide for the army. The expedition was bungled and proved a dismal failure, and Gallus laid the blame for everything on Syllaeus, who had, he declared, given him bad advice on planning the route, and had deliberately piloted the fleet into shoals and led the army through the worst stretches of desert. His object, according to Gallus, was that the Roman army should conquer the Sabaeans, but be so weakened that he could take over the kingdom himself. The theory seems very improbable.

Gallus' first error was to build a fleet of 80 warships at Cleopatris, on the Gulf of Suez, unaware that the Arabs had no warships themselves. Having wasted so much time he built 130 transports, and shipped his army across the Red Sea to Leuce Come, the southernmost town of the Nabataean kingdom. He lost several ships on the coral reefs which fringe the Arabian coast, and found the Red Sea tides very alarming. He only took a fortnight on the voyage, but many of his men were suffering from scurvy when he reached Leuce Come, and he was very indignant when he saw caravans proceeding to and from Petra without difficulty and realized that he could have reached Leuce Come by land. He spent the rest of the summer and the winter at Leuce Come to let his men recuperate, and then started southwards by land; it seems likely that the original plan had been to go by sea all the way, but Gallus had had enough of Red Sea navigation. The land march was gruelling, with long stretches of waterless desert, when water had to be carried on camels between the rare oases. At length after six months he reached the more fertile Sabaean territory, and, as Augustus says, captured three or four towns. Having failed to take Mariba, he marched back by a better route, taking only two months, and shipped his army, greatly reduced by disease, exhaustion, hunger and shipwreck, to Myos Hormos on the Egyptian Red Sea coast.

The Ethiopian expedition was not, as Augustus implies, a piece of gratuitous aggression, but was provoked by an attack of the Ethiopians, led by their warlike one-eyed queen (whose title was Candace). In 25 B.C., taking advantage of the absence of a large part of the Roman garrison of Egypt with Aelius Gallus in Arabia, they overwhelmed the three cohorts which garrisoned Syene, Philae and Elephantine on the southern frontier of Egypt, and—supreme insolence—carried off Augustus' statues as well as much booty and many prisoners. Gaius Petronius, who had been appointed to succeed Gallus when the latter left for Arabia, promptly assembled 10,000 infantry and 800 cavalry and pursued them as far as Pselchis, where, after abortive negotiations, he defeated 30,000 Ethiopians, and marched on to Nabata, the northern capital of Ethiopia, which he captured. He did not venture to go on to the southern capital Meroe, but having compelled the Ethiopians to pay tribute and left a small garrison with supplies for two years in the fortress of Primis, returned to Alexandria. Two years later the Candace attacked Primis, but Petronius was in time to relieve it. She was now willing to send an embassy to Augustus, which reached him at Samos in 22 B.C. Augustus was gracious, remitting the tribute she promised. On the other hand she ceded the northern half of the Triacontaschoenus, the Dodecaschoenus, which was henceforth held by half a dozen Roman forts.

While he was away in Spain (26–25 B.C.) Augustus tried to revive the ancient consular prerogative, obsolete for centuries, of appointing a prefect of the city to administer justice and maintain order in Rome in the consul's absence. The man appointed was Valerius Messala Corvinus, Augustus' colleague in the consulship in 31 B.C. He no doubt hoped that Messala's noble birth and former Republican sentiments would lend respectability to the newly revived office. Unfortunately Messala, having been persuaded to take the post, changed his mind and resigned after six days on the ground that he did not understand how to exercise the office, which was, he declared, unconstitutional.

In 24 B.C. Augustus at length returned to Rome, being now consul for the tenth time with Norbanus Flaccus, a noble who had supported Sextus Pompeius and Antonius in the civil wars, as his colleague. The Senate voted exceptional honours to two of his young relatives who had fought in the Spanish campaigns, his nephew Marcellus, son of his sister Octavia by her first husband, and his stepson, Tiberius Claudius Nero, Livia's elder son. Marcellus was made a senator with praetorian rank, with permission to take all offices ten years before the legal age, Tiberius to take offices five years before the legal age. Furthermore Marcellus was elected aedile forthwith, and Tiberius quaestor. The two young men were both about eighteen, so it would appear that Marcellus was Augustus' favourite; he had two years before married Julia, Augustus' only daughter (by the unloved Scribonia). The only precedent for such honours—and a close one—was the *senatus consultum* proposed by Cicero in favour of the nineteen-year-old Octavian.

Next year Augustus was consul for the eleventh time, with Terentius Varro Murena, the conqueror of the Salassi, as his colleague. Early in the year there was a political trial which caused Augustus some embarrassment. Primus, proconsul of Macedonia, was charged in the court of *maiestas* with having made war on a Thracian tribe, the Odrysae, without the Senate's authorization, and pleaded in defence that he had received orders from Augustus or alternatively Marcellus. The second allegation, which could hardly be taken seriously, nevertheless confirmed suspicions that Marcellus was being groomed to be Augustus' political heir. To the first Augustus might have replied in Cicero's words, 'all the provinces ought to be under the authority and command of the consul' (*Philippics* IV, 9) and 'the consuls are allowed by ancestral custom to enter all provinces' (*Letters to Atticus* VIII, 15, 3). Such consular authority was occasionally exercised. From the very year of the restoration of the Republic we possess a decree of the two consuls, Augustus and Agrippa, sent to the proconsul of Asia and obeyed by him as an order. But it concerns a minor and uncontentious matter, the restitution of sacred property in the provinces which had been usurped in the triumviral period, and it seems unlikely that a consul would use his superior *imperium* to impose a major decision on a proconsul. Augustus at any rate made no claim to such powers in this case. He attended the trial, and when asked by Primus' counsel, who was his fellow consul, what he was doing there and who had summoned him, replied, 'the public interest'. When asked by the praetor of the court whether he had given instructions to Primus, he denied it.

There followed a conspiracy against Augustus' life led by

Fannius Caepio, a Republican, and by Augustus' own colleague, Varro Murena. It was detected and the two leaders prosecuted in the court of *maiestas* and condemned *in absentia*: Tiberus was Caepio's accuser. Murena was succeeded as consul by Calpurnius Piso, a Republican who had fought with Brutus and Cassius. Nevertheless Augustus was alarmed at the dissatisfaction with the new regime which the trial and the conspiracy had revealed. He evidently decided that the basic cause was his unending series of consulships. At a personal level this was an irritation to the governing class. Every noble felt it his due to hold the consulship, and many rising men wanted to acquire nobility through the consulship. If there was to be one place only open to competition each year, everyone's chances were halved. But it was also contrary to the whole spirit of the Republic that one man should hold the highest office continuously. Gaius Marius had held seven consulships, but he was not a very good precedent. And Augustus now had held eleven.

Augustus had been seriously ill latterly; indeed at one moment he handed over his papers to his fellow consul Piso, and his signet ring to Agrippa. He made this the cover for his next step; it can hardly have been the real reason, for he had been delicate from childhood, and had never allowed his illnesses to impede his actions. Halfway through the year he resigned his consulship; he never held it again save on two occasions when he took it for a few weeks for family reasons. He was succeeded by Lucius Sestius, another Republican, who had been quaestor to Brutus, and still displayed his statue in his house.

This meant that he became proconsul of his own provinces (until his term ran out in 17 B.C.), and no longer had any official standing in Rome or Italy or the public provinces, and indeed could not enter Rome (he resigned outside the city) without forfeiting his *imperium*. These disabilities were partially removed by the Senate. He was exempted from the clause of the Cornelian law whereby a proconsul forfeited his *imperium* on entering the *pomoerium*. This of course did not give him the right to exercise his *imperium* in the city, or indeed anywhere except in his own province, but it enabled him to attend the Senate and take part in meetings of the people. He was furthermore granted a *maius imperium* over other proconsuls, so that he could issue them orders and enter their provinces freely. It was a striking addition to Augustus' powers for, as stated above, even as consul his powers over the public provinces had been shadowy, and it is somewhat surprising that the Senate conceded it at this juncture. Augustus may have asked for it in view of his forthcoming general tour of his provinces.

Finally Augustus was accorded the powers of a tribune of the plebs for life. He already had the sacrosanctity of a tribune (since 36 B.C.) and an extended power of *auxilium* (since 30 B.C.). He now received the full powers, including the veto, the right of proposing plebiscites, and the right of summoning the Senate and eliciting from it *senatus consulta*. The last right was felt to be inadequate, or at any rate undignified for a person of Augustus' standing, for tribunes had a very low precedence in convening the Senate, ranking below consuls and praetors, and a special right of convening the Senate was accordingly granted to Augustus. These were convenient powers, which enabled Augustus to fulfil his political role at Rome, but he made remarkably little use of them. He is never known to have exercised his veto. He passed a few laws, but more often got the consuls to legislate for him. All the known *senatus consulta* of his reign were initiated by the consuls. On the other hand he gave the tribunician power a prominent place in his titulature, using it to date the years of his reign. One may suspect that he asked for it not so much for its practical usefulness as for its popular appeal. If the nobility grudged him his magisterial powers, he could base his position on the support of the plebs.

In this year Augustus transferred Gallia Narbonensis and Cyprus from his own rule to that of the Senate. This was to demonstrate that he would keep his provinces only so long as they required military protection. It also provided two provinces for the two extra praetors which he created for the treasury this year.

In this same year Augustus asked the Senate to confer a consular *imperium* for ten years on Agrippa, and to assign him the same provinces as to himself. Agrippa went to the East, and made Mytilene on the island of Lesbos his headquarters: his later activities show that his powers extended over the West as well and that he enjoyed a *maius imperium* over other proconsuls. This move is attributed by Suetonius and Dio to personal motives, that Agrippa was jealous of the honours given to Marcellus and went off in a huff, or that he tactfully withdrew to avoid a possible clash with Marcellus. A modern version is that a resentful Agrippa extorted the appointment from the unwilling Augustus. These romantic versions seem improbable, for there is no evidence whatever that Agrippa was ever discontented with his position or disloyal to his great friend; he was a man of very humble birth and no doubt grateful for three consulships. Another modern view is that the appointment was a further attempt to please the Republicans, by making the consular *imperium* collegiate. There may be some truth in this. Augustus takes credit in the *Res Gestae* (6) for having five times asked for a colleague in the tribunician power, and the same may have applied to the consular *imperium*, which he avoids mentioning in the *Res Gestae*. But it seems most probable that Augustus wished to ensure that the armies would be in reliable hands in case his next illness proved fatal. If Marcellus was the cause of trouble between Augustus and Agrippa, it was quickly removed. Before the year was out he was dead, despite the treatment of Augustus' doctor, Antonius Musa.

Next year (22 B.C.) the consuls Claudius Marcellus and Lucius Arruntius, both nobles, proved very inadequate to the situation. The people of Rome resented the removal of Augustus from the consulship, and their feelings were exacerbated by floods in Rome, a plague in Italy and a shortage of corn. They demanded that Augustus be given a perpetual and annual consulship, or a dictatorship, and besieged the Senate in the senate house until they agreed. They also pressed upon him the censorship, and a curatorship of the corn supply. He accepted the last office only, and remedied the shortage in a few days. He also had two censors elected, but they achieved nothing.

He then left Rome for Sicily, where he planted veteran colonies at Syracuse and other cities, presumably on the land confiscated after the defeat of Sextus Pompeius. Next spring

(21 B.C.) he moved on to Greece where he rewarded Sparta with the island of Cythera for taking his side in the Actium war, and deprived Athens of Aegina and Eretria for being on the wrong side. He passed the winter at Samos and in the following year (20 B.C.) regulated the affairs of Asia and Bithynia-Pontus; he was making full use of his *maius imperium*. He deprived the free city of Cyzicus of its liberty for having allowed some Roman citizens to be killed in a riot, and adjusted the taxes of various cities. He next moved on to Syria, where he deprived Tyre and Sidon of their liberty, and restored various minor client kings whom he had deposed after Actium. He also, on the death of Zenodorus, the tetrarch of the Ituraeans, partitioned his principality. Part of it had already four years ago been given to Herod, who had done excellent work in suppressing the brigandage endemic in the area; he now got two more districts, and other parts were allocated to Tyre and Sidon, while the religious centre of the Ituraeans, Heliopolis, was assigned to Berytus, which became a veteran colony.

This same year Augustus achieved a diplomatic triumph. Roman public opinion had ever since Actium been expecting that he would avenge the defeats inflicted by the Parthians on Crassus and Antonius, recover the rebellious client kingdom of Armenia, and in vaguer terms conquer the East: 'May the Capitol stand resplendent,' wrote Horace (*Odes* III, iii, 42–4) 'and fierce Rome triumph over the Medes and impose on them her laws.' It is evident that Augustus had no ambitions for Eastern conquests, and fully realized how dangerous an operation an invasion of Parthia was. But he realized that he must do something to satisfy Roman public opinion and restore Roman prestige in the East. Armenia, though of no value, economic or strategic, to Rome, was unfortunately a point of prestige. Pompeius had conquered Tigranes and restored him to his throne, and the Roman government could not abandon its suzerainty without loss of face. As for Parthia, a more symbolic submission would suffice —the surrender of the Roman prisoners and standards lost by Crassus and Antonius.

Augustus had some useful counters for the game; Tigranes, the younger brother of king Artaxes of Armenia, who had been captured by Antonius and had been living since 30 B.C. at Rome, and Tiridates, a brother and rival of king Phraates of Parthia, who had also been living in Roman territory since 30 B.C., and Phraates, son of king Phraates, whom Tiridates had kidnapped. We do not know the details of the negotiations, but in response to a request from king Phraates Augustus had in 21 B.C. sent back his son, on condition that the standards and the prisoners were returned. When nothing happened Augustus ordered Tiberius (who was only twenty-one) to bring up troops from Illyricum. Faced by a double threat from Tiberius in Asia Minor and Augustus in Syria, Phraates promptly surrendered the standards and prisoners. Tiberius marched on into Armenia, where he met with no resistance. King Artaxes was murdered by the pro-Roman party in the Armenian nobility, and Tiberius solemnly crowned Tigranes. These successes were celebrated by a great issue of coins bearing such legends as *civibus et signis militaribus a Parthis recuperatis* and *Armenia recepta*.

This done, Augustus went back to Samos to spend the winter. He received an embassy from India, and he rewarded the Samians for their hospitality by a grant of freedom. Meanwhile at Rome the troubles had gone on. After Augustus left for Sicily in 22 there were disorders at the consular elections, the assembly insisting on electing only one consul, Marcus Lollius, when Augustus refused to stand. The Senate begged him to return, but he refused. He must have felt a certain satisfaction at the difficulties in which the nobles were involved. They had forced him to resign the consulship and retire to his provinces, leaving them in charge of Rome and Italy. They had found even that task too much for them, and Augustus was determined to impress that lesson on their minds.

Eventually Aemilius Lepidus was elected to the second consulship, but next year (21) a similar crisis arose. Augustus relented so far as to send Agrippa—there could have been no more distasteful choice to the nobility—to Rome. At the same time he arranged that Agrippa should divorce his wife, Octavia's daughter Marcella, and marry Julia, recently widowed by Marcellus' death: Agrippa was to be more closely linked to his chief's family. He succeeded in getting two consuls, Marcus Appuleius and Publius Silius, elected for next year, and then left for Gaul and Spain, where the Astures had rebelled again. The troubles then revived and the people once more insisted on electing one consul only, reserving the other place for Augustus.

The year 19 B.C. opened with one consul, Sentius Saturninus. There were riotous scenes at the elections. When he tried to reject the nominations of some candidates for the quaestorship whom he considered unworthy of that office, they contumaciously insisted on standing, despite his threats that he would exert his consular powers to punish them if they did. Even more contumacious was Egnatius Rufus, who having made himself very popular in his aedileship, had stood for the praetorship and won it the next year, contrary to the law, and was now standing for the consulship immediately after his praetorship. The Senate in view of the grave situation passed the *senatus consultum ultimum*, and Egnatius Rufus was executed, but the situation remained menacing, and an embassy was sent to Augustus urgently begging him to return. Augustus nominated one of the senatorial envoys, Quintus Lucretius, who had been one of the proscribed, as Saturninus' colleague, and journeyed in leisurely fashion to Rome, arriving on 12 October. The Senate expressed its thankfulness by sending the new consul Quintus Lucretius with several of the praetors and tribunes down to Campania to greet him, by declaring 12 October an annual public holiday, and by dedicating an altar to Fortuna Redux. They also gave Tiberius, who was now twenty-three, praetorian rank, and his younger brother Drusus the right to hold magistracies five years before the legal age. Finally they gave Augustus himself a new constitutional power. It was, according to Dio (LIV, 10, 5), 'the *imperium* of the consuls for life, so that he should use the twelve *fasces* always and everywhere and should sit on his curule chair between the consuls for the time being'. It is usually held that by this Dio merely means the consular prerogative of having twelve lictors and the right to sit between the consuls, on the ground that Augustus must have mentioned a consular *imperium* for life in the *Res Gestae* if he had possessed it. This is a weak argument, since Augustus carefully avoids mentioning even his provincial *imperium*—no one could guess from the *Res Gestae* that he had been proconsul of half the Empire for forty years with *maius imperium* over the other half. He only mentions *imperium* three times, once when he first obtained it in 43 B.C. (1), and then in 8 B.C. and A.D. 14, when he conducted censuses in Italy 'with consular *imperium*' (8). Moreover Augustus dearly loves to record in full all titular honours, and would surely have mentioned the grant of the twelve fasces and the seat between consuls had it been an empty honour.

The strongest argument, however, that Augustus received the consular *imperium* for life is that he henceforth exercised it in Italy and in Rome itself. Since 23 B.C. his *imperium* had been confined to his provinces—with a *maius imperium* in other provinces. Henceforth we find him maintaining his praetorian cohorts near Rome, calling up citizens in Italy, carrying out the census, exercising jurisdiction, civil and criminal, banishing Roman citizens (amongst them Ovid) from Italy. He received the names of the candidates for the consular and praetorian elections, a specifically consular prerogative, and once again, having last done so when consul in 26 B.C., nominated a prefect of the city, Statilius Taurus, when he left Rome for Gaul in 16 B.C.

Augustus' constitutional powers were now complete: he received two additions to his titles later, *pontifex maximus* and *pater patriae*, but these were purely honorific and added nothing to his powers. In addition to his consular *imperium* over his own provinces and his *maius imperium* over the public provinces, he now had the *imperium* of a consul over Italy and Rome. All these powers were studiously veiled. Later emperors might call themselves proconsul in their provinces, but Augustus never did. In the *Res Gestae* Augustus never alluded to his (or his colleagues') consular power or to his (or their) *maius imperium*. He mentions his consular *imperium* in Italy twice, to explain under what authority he held his second and third censuses—the first he held as consul.

The tribunician power, which had never been of much practical use, now became purely symbolic, the *summi fastigi vocabulum* ('title of the highest eminence': Tacitus, *Annals* III, 56) which appears on every inscription and is given as a supreme honour to a colleague to mark his promotion to equal status with Augustus himself. The concentration of so much *imperium* into the hands of one man would, it would seem, have marred the picture of the restored Republic, but the popular powers of a tribune of the plebs might be held for life without offence.

5

The Principate

W HEN in the consulships of Marcus Vinicius and Quintus
Lucretius (19 B.C.) and Publius and Gnaeus Lentulus
(18 B.C.) and Paulus Fabius Maximus and Quintus Tubero
(11 B.C.) the Senate and people agreed that I should be
created sole curator of laws and morals with supreme
powers, I accepted no magistracy contrary to the custom of
our ancestors.

So wrote Augustus in his *Res Gestae* (6). Dio on the other
hand says that in 19 B.C. the Senate offered Augustus a *cura
morum* and a *censoria potestas* with extravagant powers,
including that of enacting, apparently by his sole authority,
Augustan laws, to which all the Senate would swear
obedience. Augustus refused the extravagant powers but
accepted a simple *cura morum* and *censoria potestas* for five
years. Dio has generally been accused of inaccuracy, but the
two statements are perfectly compatible, though, if Dio is
correct, Augustus is rather disingenuous. For though he does
not say he refused a simple grant of censorial powers, he does
imply it. Censorial powers, like the consular *imperium*, were
something that Augustus liked to keep in the background—
he fails to mention that he had held them in 28 B.C. for his
first census and purge of the Senate.

Next year (18 B.C.) he used his censorial powers to hold a
second revision of the roll of the Senate, intending to reduce it
to 300, the number of the old Senate that had withstood
Hannibal. As on the first occasion he tried to get the senators
to select themselves. He started the process by nominating
thirty on oath, they each nominated five, one of whom was
selected by lot to be senator, and nominated another five and
so on. Augustus soon however detected corruption, and had
to make the selection himself. He only succeeded in reducing
the figure to 600.

It was in this year too that Augustus, responding to popular demand, initiated his programme of moral reform, promulgating a number of laws in virtue of his tribunician power, a *lex Iulia de adulteriis coercendis* penalizing adultery and other irregular sexual relations, a *lex Iulia de maritandis ordinibus* to encourage marriage and the procreation of children, a *lex Iulia de ambitu* to curb electoral corruption, and a *lex Iulia sumptuaria* to check extravagance and luxury.

The next year (17 B.C.) to purify the Roman people of its past sins and to inaugurate the new age, the *xv viri sacris faciundis*, of which Augustus and Agrippa were members, celebrated with great splendour and solemnity the Secular Games. These were an expiatory ceremony which, according to the commonest tradition, were celebrated every century and had last taken place in 149 B.C., having been omitted in 49 B.C. owing to the civil war. The *xv viri*, however, after an investigation by the learned lawyer Ateius Capito, decided that the last celebration was in 126 B.C. and that the proper interval was 110 years.

The traditional festival was a gloomy day of atonement, in which sacrifices were offered by night to the infernal gods, Dis and Proserpina. In the Augustan celebration the emphasis was shifted to hope for the coming age, with daytime sacrifices to Jupiter and Juno and Apollo and Diana. Horace was commissioned to write the hymn, which was sung by twenty-seven boys and twenty-seven girls.

In the same year Augustus adopted the two sons that Julia had borne to Agrippa, the elder of whom was three and the younger one. They thus became Gaius Julius Caesar and Lucius Julius Caesar respectively. The succession was thus clearly indicated. If Augustus should die Agrippa, possessing the *imperium consulare* and the *tribunicia potestas*, would automatically step into his place, but only as caretaker for his two sons, who were of the blood of Caesar and now sons of Augustus. In 18 B.C., as the term of his province would run out in the following year, Augustus had it renewed, but for five years only, and not only had Agrippa's consular *imperium* renewed for the same period, but had the tribunician power conferred on him for five years. Next year Agrippa went to Syria and accepted an invitation from King Herod to pay a visit to his kingdom. Herod entertained him lavishly, and proudly displayed to him the new cities that he had built, Caesarea and Sebaste in honour of Augustus, and Agrippias in honour of his guest.

In the autumn Agrippa moved to Asia, whence he was soon called away to settle the affairs of the kingdom of Bosporus. This kingdom had for long been ruled by Asander, who was married to Dynamis, the daughter of Pharnaces and granddaughter of the great Mithradates VI of Pontus. In 17 B.C. he was overthrown by a rebel named Scribonius, who married his widow. Agrippa at first thought it sufficient to order Polemo king of Pontus to eject the usurper, but the people of Bosporus refused to receive Polemo. Agrippa was obliged to intervene himself, and collecting a fleet sailed to Sinope, where he was joined by King Herod with his fleet. Polemo was successfully installed and married to Dynamis. The settlement did not however last long. Dynamis quarrelled with her new husband and raised a rebellion against him with the aid of a Sarmatian chieftain Aspurgus, and eventually in 8 B.C. Polemo was killed, and Dynamis and Aspurgus became rulers of Bosporus. She called herself 'friend of the Roman people', however, and furnished contingents to the imperial army.

Having installed Polemo in Bosporus, Agrippa, accompanied by Herod, made, in virtue of his *maius imperium*, a considerable stay in the province of Asia, and on Herod's prompting issued a number of edicts protecting the privileges of the local Jews.

Augustus had meanwhile been called to Gaul by the news that one of his legates, Marcus Lollius, had been defeated by two German tribes, the Usipetes and the Tencteri. He took Tiberius with him, although he was praetor in that year (16 B.C.). The defeat, however, proved not to be serious, and the tribes promptly submitted and gave hostages. Augustus was thus able to spend the year in overhauling the finances of Gaul. He had made one of his freedmen, Licinus, his financial agent (*procurator*) for the Gallic provinces; Licinus was himself a Gaul, enslaved by Julius Caesar and inherited by his adoptive son. Licinus had apparently been guilty of some sharp practices; he had for instance exacted fourteen monthly instalments of tribute per annum by adding two more months to the calendar after the tenth month, December. Augustus was so pleased with his financial results, however, that he retained him in his post.

There was much fighting on the northern frontier this year. Silius, apparently the proconsul of Illyricum, had to fight the Noricans and the Pannonians and a Thracian tribe, the Dentheletae, to the north and northeast and east of his province, and also to suppress two Alpine tribes, the Camuni and the Venones. In the course of these operations he subdued and annexed the kingdom of Noricum.

It may have been the general unrest on the northern and northeastern frontiers of Italy that determined Augustus to embark on a systematic reduction of the area. It was in the first place absurd that the mountain tribes of the Alps were still unsubdued and could and did raid the plains of northern Italy and exact blackmail from travellers using the Alpine passes. In the second place, though Augustus had himself before Actium conquered Dalmatia, the tribes were still restive and the area was subject to invasions from the interior. Moreover the coastal road down to Dyrrachium was a very difficult one, and the shortest and easiest route from northern Italy to the East was through the land of the Pannonians along the valley of the Save, and thence through Thrace. Conditions in Thrace were tolerably stable. The two most powerful tribal dynasties, those of the Sapaei on the Aegean and the Astae on the Black Sea had recently been united by marriage, and the new dynasty controlled most, if not all, the other tribes, though not very firmly. In this very year Claudius Marcellus had had to subdue the Bessi, who had rebelled against the Thracian king, and five years later in 11 B.C. Piso, the legate of Galatia, had to be summoned from his province to suppress another revolt of the Bessi.

In 15 B.C. Tiberius and his younger brother Drusus systematically subdued Raetia and Vindelicia and the central Alps. Next year the Maritime Alps were reduced. On the trophy which was set up to Augustus a few years later in the Maritime Alps were enumerated the forty-eight tribes which had been conquered: these did not include fifteen tribes subject to King Cottius, who had made a timely submission, nor those of the kingdom of Noricum. The acquired territory, which extended up to the upper Danube, was for a few years assigned to an imperial legate, but soon divided into districts—the Maritime Alps, Raetia and Vindelicia, Noricum—and put under military governors, usually ex-centurions, with the title of prefect. When King Cottius died his son Donnus ruled his father's kingdom as prefect.

In 14 B.C., despite all the wars which he had on hand, Augustus had to discharge a large number of men who had signed on for sixteen years after Actium. As in 30 B.C., he planted these in colonies, probably mostly in the provinces: he is recorded to have founded colonies in Spain and Gaul at this time. Once again he paid for the land out of his own pocket. Next year (13 B.C.) he returned to Rome and was honoured with the famous *Ara Pacis* (see Chapter 14). Agrippa also returned from the East, and Tiberius was consul for the first time this year (at the age of twenty-nine). Augustus and Agrippa had their provinces renewed for five years, and Agrippa also had his tribunician power extended for the same period, and was sent to fight the Pannonians. He did not reach Pannonia till late in the year, rapidly restored order and returned to Italy. Here he fell ill and died in Campania. It was a heavy blow to Augustus. Agrippa had been his devoted friend since their schooldays, and was probably the only man in whom he could absolutely trust. He had won most of his important wars for him, but had been content to remain a subordinate, even when officially raised to be Augustus' colleague and honoured with the hand of his only daughter. Augustus gave him a magnificent state funeral and buried him in his own mausoleum.

The nobles boycotted the funeral games. It is not very easy to see why they should have hated Agrippa so venomously. He possessed some qualities which excused even the humblest birth. He was a great general and singularly modest in accepting triumphs for his victories; and if he acquired a considerable fortune, including estates in Sicily and Egypt, and the old public, formerly Attalid, lands in the Thracian Chersonnese, he spent it munificently, building the Pantheon and the Saepta Iulia, and a public baths, which he left to the Roman people with endowments to provide free entry, and two aqueducts, the Julia and the Virgo. He was, however, it would seem, a dour character, and no doubt took little pains to ingratiate himself with the nobility. But probably the nobles canalized against Augustus' alter ego all their repressed resentment against Augustus himself and the new regime.

In 12 B.C. Augustus achieved one of his great ambitions. Lepidus, the former triumvir, died the year before, and Augustus was elected to succeed him as *pontifex maximus*. The crowds that assembled from all Italy for the election were, he proudly boasted, unprecedented.

The very next year (11 B.C.) Tiberius was compelled to divorce his wife Vipsania, Agrippa's daughter, to whom he was deeply attached, and marry Julia. He was then despatched to Dalmatia, which, as it had proved by no means a peaceful province, was surrendered by the Senate to Augustus' care. He continued to campaign against the Dalmatians and Pannonians until 9 B.C., when the conquest of the area was deemed complete. It was formed into two provinces, the original Illyricum and east of it Pannonia up to the Danube from Vindobona to Singidunum. Meanwhile, Drusus was campaigning in Germany east of the Rhine up to the Elbe. He died in 9 B.C. and Tiberius took over for a year. When he left Germany next year (7 B.C.) to receive a triumph and a second consulship, he had, according to his admirer Velleius, 'so tamed it as almost to have reduced it to the form of a tributary province'. This clearly means that regular administration and taxation had not yet been attempted.

Meanwhile at home Augustus, having received censorial powers again, held a third review of the roll of the Senate in 11 B.C.; nothing but the bare fact is recorded. He also set up a permanent commission for the maintenance and management of the aqueducts of Rome. Agrippa had not only built two new aqueducts and virtually rebuilt the others, but had ever since his aedileship in 34 B.C. maintained them at his own expense with a gang of 240 slaves. These he had left to Augustus, who gave them to the state. *Senatus consulta* and a law were passed setting up a permanent commission of one consular, one praetorian and one junior senator, to be elected by the Senate on the proposal of Augustus, and allocating to them the necessary staff and funds. The first consular curator, who held office until A.D. 13, was the Valerius Messala Corvinus who had resigned the prefecture of the city in 25 B.C. In 8 B.C. Augustus held a second census, in virtue of his consular *imperium*, in which 4,233,600 citizens were counted. It is unfortunately impossible to say how much of the considerable rise was due to natural increase, how much to grants of citizenship, and how much to manumission of slaves. This year Augustus' provincial command was renewed again, this time for another ten years, and the month of Sextilis, in which Augustus had entered on his first consulate and had annexed Egypt and had ended the civil wars, was changed to August.

Maecenas died this year. While Augustus was grieved at the loss of an old friend, who had done much to assist his rise to power from the very beginning down to Actium, the blow was probably not so great as Agrippa's death. Maecenas' proud refusal to accept senatorial rank meant that no important employment was open to him under the restored Republic. If contemporary gossip is true, he had in 23 B.C. betrayed to his wife Terentia that the conspiracy of her brother Terentius Varro Murena was known to Augustus, and had as a result fallen into disgrace. If so the estrangement was not lasting. Later Augustus is said to have seduced the beautiful Terentia, but this again does not seem to have interrupted the old friendship.

In the year following his second consulship Tiberius was given the tribunician power for five years and consular *imperium* over Augustus' provinces; he had hitherto commanded only as *legatus Augusti pro praetore*. Augustus wished him to go to Armenia, where he had fourteen years before installed a client king. This king, Tigranes II, had died, and his son Tigranes III and his daughter Erato had seized the throne without the permission of Rome. Tiberius refused to go, and begged to be relieved of his public duties and retire to Rhodes. Augustus was much annoyed, but let him go.

The reason for this sudden quarrel was the promotion of Gaius and Lucius Caesar. They were only fourteen and eleven respectively, and apparently very spoilt and ill-mannered boys, but Augustus doted on the two heirs of his body. It had already been suggested that Gaius should be elected consul, and Augustus, while professing to be shocked at this constitutional anomaly, was obviously delighted. Next year (5 B.C.) he took the consulship (his twelfth) himself to lead Gaius into the Forum, and the Senate and people enthusiastically voted that he should be designated consul forthwith, to enter on office in five years' time when he would be twenty, and should meanwhile attend the Senate. He was also made *pontifex*, and the equestrian order proclaimed him *princeps iuventutis*. The same ritual was repeated for Lucius in 2 B.C., when Augustus became consul for the thirteenth and last time, except that Lucius became an augur. In this year Augustus was acclaimed as father of his country by the plebs, the equestrian order and the Senate. Their unanimous desire was conveyed to Augustus by Valerius Massala, who had fought for the Republic at Philippi.

His pleasure at this high tribute was abruptly destroyed by the scandal of Julia. Julia had for some years past been following the precepts of Ovid's *Art of Love*, but Augustus was naturally the last to hear of it. It was impossible for the author of the *lex Iulia de adulteriis* to connive at the scandal, which was flagrant, and Julia and a number of her lovers were brought to trial. She was banished to the island of Pandateria off the coast of Campania. The most prominent of her lovers, Antonius Iullus, son of the triumvir, who had risen to be consul in 10 B.C., either committed suicide or was executed, perhaps for treason. Four other nobles were exiled to islands.

In 1 B.C. Gaius Caesar, who would be consul when he reached the age of twenty in the following year, was given the consular *imperium* in order to settle the Armenian and Parthian problem. After Tiberius' retirement five years before, a Roman nominee named Artavasdes had been installed on the Armenian throne with Roman troops, but he had soon been expelled by the Parthians and Tigranes had returned; nothing had since been done to restore Roman honour. In view of his youth Gaius was given an unofficial adviser in the person of Marcus Lollius. He proceeded in a leisurely fashion, visiting the provinces and armies along the Danube, traversing Asia Minor and then turning south to Syria, where he entered upon his consulship in A.D. 1, and even visiting Egypt.

Gaius had perhaps been instructed to wait until negotiations already under way between Augustus and Phraataces the Parthian king and Tigranes the Armenian usurper bore fruit. Next year a ceremonial conference was held between Gaius and Phraataces on neutral ground on an island in the Euphrates. We are not informed of the terms of the agreement, but, Tigranes having died, Gaius declared Ariobarzanes, king of Media, king of Armenia. There was some resistance in the country, however, to the new king. Gaius was wounded during the fighting and asked to be allowed to return to Rome. He died on the way at Limyra in Lycia on 21 February A.D. 4. His brother Lucius had already died at Massilia on 20 August A.D. 2.

King Ariobarzanes shortly died, and his son Artavasdes was killed. Augustus thereupon installed a certain Tigranes whom he describes as sprung from the royal line of Armenia. He was actually the son of Herod's son Alexander and Glaphyra, daughter of Archelaus, king of Cappadocia. His reign seems also to have been brief, and Erato, sister of the usurper Tigranes, was queen for a brief while. Finally in A.D. 11 to 12 Vonones, a Parthian king who had lost his throne, seized that of Armenia.

Tiberius had returned from Rhodes to Rome in A.D. 2, shortly before Lucius' death. But though allowed to live in Rome, he was still under Augustus' displeasure. His consular *imperium* and tribunician power, which had run out in 1 B.C., were not renewed, and he was not offered any military command. But with the death of Gaius everything changed. He was now the only surviving male member of the family of Augustus besides Germanicus, the son of Drusus, who was only sixteen, his younger brother Claudius Nero, who was at this time considered to be mentally defective, and the third and posthumous son of Agrippa and Julia, also called Agrippa, who was fourteen. Augustus was obliged to rely on Tiberius, and he adopted him as his son, declaring in a public statement that he did so 'for reasons of state' (Suetonius, *Tiberius* 21, 3). Malicious persons interpreted this remark as meaning 'despite his personal aversion', but there is no reason to believe that Augustus did not mean what he said. This adoption was not a mere family affair, but implied that

Tiberius was Augustus' political heir. In accordance with this Augustus at the same time had Tiberius' consular *imperium* and tribunician power renewed for ten years. Tiberius, although he already had a son of his own by Vipsania, Drusus, had on Augustus' request shortly before adopted his nephew, Germanicus, who was thus also brought into the Julian family. This was one of Augustus' ingenious dynastic schemes. Germanicus' mother was Antonia, daughter of Marcus Antonius and Augustus' sister Octavia, and had moreover married Agrippina, daughter of Agrippa and Augustus' daughter Julia. It was clearly intended that Tiberius should be succeeded by Germanicus of the Octavian family and he by a son who would be a descendant of Augustus himself. Augustus also adopted Agrippa. He was still hankering for an heir of his body, but as Agrippa grew up he became so wild and violent that eventually in A.D. 7 the Senate banished him to an island.

During these family troubles the administration of the Empire and the defence of its frontiers had gone on. In 4 B.C. King Herod had died and the fate of his kingdom had been settled. Herod in the latter part of his life fell under Augustus' displeasure. In the course of a dispute with Obodas, king of Arabia, he had in 10 B.C. invaded Arabian territory—or as Herod represented the affair, made a punitive raid to destroy a nest of brigands who were ravaging his territory. Augustus had strong ideas about the duty of client kings to keep the peace with their neighbours, and wrote to Herod that he could no longer regard him as a friend.

The other cause for disquiet was the bitter feuds between Herod's sons, who accused one another of treason and exacerbated their father's naturally suspicious temper with fatal results to themselves. 'It is preferable,' as Augustus remarked (Macrobius, *Saturnalia* II, 4), 'to be Herod's pig than Herod's son' (the remark was probably made in Greek, in which 'pig' is a pun on 'son'). Alexander and Aristobulus, originally his favourites, the sons of the Hasmonaean Mariamne, were brought under suspicion by their elder brother Antipater, and in 12 B.C. Herod took them to Italy to be tried by Augustus himself. Augustus acquitted them and temporarily reconciled the family, but five years later the quarrel came to a head

71

again. Augustus advised Herod to have the two young men tried before a Roman court at the colony of Berytus. This court, consisting of the legate of Syria with numerous assessors, found Alexander and Aristobulus guilty, and Herod executed them. Antipater, however, did not long enjoy his triumph. He was brought to trial before Quintilius Varus, the legate of Syria, in Jerusalem, being charged by Herod and Nicolaus of Damascus with attempted parricide. Varus returned to Antioch without publicly pronouncing sentence. Not long afterwards Herod fell seriously ill, and a few days before he died signed Antipater's death warrant, and made a fresh will in which he appointed Archelaus king of Samaria, Judaea and Idumaea, and Antipas and Philip tetrarchs under his suzerainty of Galilee and Peraea and of the Ituraean districts respectively.

All three sons went up to Rome to dispute the succession, and so did delegations from the Greek cities of the kingdom and of the Jewish community, who wanted direct provincial rule. There were serious riots at Jerusalem and even rebellions while they were away, to suppress which Varus, the legate of Syria, had to use three legions and 1500 veterans from Berytus besides contingents from Aretas of Arabia and other client kings. Augustus decided to maintain Herod's will in principle. Archelaus, however, was not to be king but ethnarch and to have no jurisdiction over the tetrarchies of his brothers. The Greek cities were to be incorporated in the province of Syria.

There was yet another revision of the senatorial roll in this period, in A.D. 4. This time Augustus at last succeeded in getting the Senate to purge itself by a committee of three senators chosen by lot from ten nominated by himself. In the same year there was an abortive conspiracy by Cornelius Cinna Magnus, a grandson of the great Pompeius. He was pardoned and became consul next year.

During the years that Tiberius had been absent, fighting had been going on on the northern fronts. In default of any member of the imperial family of suitable age Augustus had used senators as his legates, some like Domitius Ahenobarbus nobles, but the majority new men who had risen in the triumviral period and since. The most notable achievement of this period was the conquest and pacification of the province of Moesia, which comprised the territory south of the Danube from the boundary of Pannonia eastwards to the Oescus. The province was at first, like the Alpine districts, placed under an ex-centurion prefect of the tribes of Moesia and Treballia, but later under a consular legate and its boundary advanced to the Black Sea. It was certainly in existence in A.D. 6 and probably already in 1 B.C., when Gaius Caesar seems to have traversed this area on his way to the East. The Dacians, north of the Danube, also made their submission. Moesia screened Macedonia and the Thracian kingdom from barbarian attack, and it was probably now that the proconsul of Macedonia lost his legions.

When Tiberius was received back into favour in A.D. 4 he was promptly despatched to Gaul, where he spent that year and the next completing the reduction of Germany up the Elbe. In A.D. 6 he was transferred to Pannonia to take charge of the great campaign which was planned for that year. Some years before the Marcomanni had decided to migrate from their old home in the area which was now under Roman control to a more distant and secure land, Bohemia. There under the king Maroboduus they had established themselves and even built up a little empire of subject peoples. This German Empire was considered to be a threat to the Roman Empire. It moreover blocked the way to a grand strategic scheme for establishing a frontier running up the Elbe from the Baltic to Bohemia and thence either southwards to the Danube at Carnuntum, or more ambitiously eastwards to the Black Sea, taking in the Dacians.

A double attack was launched by Tiberius from Pannonia and by Sentius Saturninus from southern Germany. The Roman armies had entered Bohemia, when news came of a great uprising in Dalmatia and Pannonia. Maroboduus was fortunately willing to make peace on being recognized as a friend and ally of the Roman people, and Tiberius was able to return to his province, where he found that the legate of Moesia had already marched in with his legions, supported by the forces of Rhoemetalces king of Thrace. The revolt was checked, but it took four years of stubborn and ruthless fighting before it was finally crushed in A.D. 9.

At Rome there was at first a panic. Augustus tried to raise more troops in Italy, but without great success. Recruiting among citizens was so bad that he had to fall back on freedmen, and on slaves levied from their owners and freed. With these men he created *cohortes civium Romanorum ingenuorum* for the recruits of free birth and *cohortes civium Romanorum voluntariorum* for those of servile origin.

It was also in A.D. 6 that the problem of soldiers' discharge bounties was finally solved. Since the last big discharge in 14 B.C. Augustus had been releasing men in small numbers year by year, in 7 and 6, and 4, 3 and 2 B.C. He now did not buy land for them, but gave them bounties in cash. Since 2 B.C., there had been no discharges, and Augustus decided that he could not go on indefinitely paying bounties or buying land out of his own pocket. He therefore proposed the establishment of a military treasury for this purpose, to be managed by three prefects of praetorian rank to be chosen by lot. Augustus himself gave 170,000,000 sesterces to start the fund and client kings and free cities also contributed. But a regular revenue was required, and Augustus invited senators to send in suggestions. When none of these proved adequate, he proposed two new taxes on Roman citizens, a five per cent tax on inheritances and a one per cent tax on sales. The former was a very moderate tax, particularly as fortunes below 100,000 sesterces were exempt, and so were inheritances and bequests from near relatives, but it was received with much grumbling. The maximum length of service had been raised the year before to sixteen years for praetorians and twenty for legionaries. The discharge bounties were fixed at 5000 denarii for praetorians and 3000 denarii for legionaries.

In the same year the problem of the Roman fire service was finally solved. Augustus had in 22 B.C. put a corps of 600 public slaves at the disposal of the aediles, who were supposed, among their many other duties, to suppress fires, but this proved unsatisfactory. He now enrolled seven cohorts, a thousand strong, from freedmen, and allocated two of the fourteen regions into which he had divided the city to a cohort. In charge he put an equestrian prefect, the *praefectus vigilum*. This was the first case in which Augustus took into his own hands a part of the administration of Rome. Next year a new tax on Roman citizens of four per cent on the sale of slaves was instituted to pay for the *vigiles*. The *vigiles*, it may be noted, were not merely firefighters, but patrolled the city by night, and developed into a police force which dealt with burglary and other nocturnal crimes.

In these two years there was a severe famine in Rome. At the last serious crisis in 22 B.C. Augustus had on the urgent demand of the people accepted a *cura annonae* himself, which he only held for a few weeks. He had later arranged that two ex-praetors should be annually elected to supervise the distribution. Four years later he had modified this scheme: four ex-praetors were to be chosen by lot from a panel nominated by all the magistrates of the year. He now had a special appointment made of two consulars in A.D. 6 and 7, but their function was still apparently only to distribute the corn available. This crisis may have impelled Augustus to seek a more satisfactory solution for the problem. The distribution of the ration could be left to annually appointed senators. The real problem was the procurement of corn, whether by compulsory purchase as in Sicily or as tax in kind as in Egypt, and the creation of sufficient stocks to tide over emergencies. Before the end of the reign this duty had been assigned to an equestrian officer, the *praefectus annonae*.

Also in A.D. 6 Archelaus, ethnarch of Judaea, was deposed. Both his Jewish and his Samaritan subjects complained bitterly of his oppressive rule, and his two brothers supported their charges. The case was heard at Rome by Augustus, and Archelaus was banished to Vienna in Gallia Narbonensis, and his kingdom annexed. It was rather an awkward problem, being remote from Antioch, where the legate of Syria normally resided; the Jews were notoriously a restive and difficult people, and the administration was moreover a centralized one, modelled on that of Egypt, and not capable of running itself under remote control, as were the cities of which most provinces were composed. The annexed kingdom was therefore placed under an equestrian prefect, who could at the same time run the complicated administrative machine and keep a close eye on local security. There were three prefects under Augustus, but nothing is known of them except their names.

Another client king was in trouble. The Gaetulians rose against Juba of Mauretania, and he had to ask help from Cornelius Cossus, the proconsul of Africa, the only proconsul who now had a legion. Cossus was successful and took the cognomen of Gaetulicus, and received triumphal ornaments —triumphs were by now reserved to Augustus' family. Sardinia proved too much for its proconsuls owing to its persistent brigandage, and was handed over to Augustus, who governed it through equestrian officers with the title of *pro legato*. A province hitherto governed by a proconsul could hardly be handed over to a mere prefect, but was not worthy of a senatorial *legatus*, so the prefect was given the acting rank of legate.

In this year Tiberius announced final victory in Dalmatia and Pannonia. The Senate voted two triumphal arches in Pannonia and a triumph for Augustus and Tiberius, and various honours to Germanicus and Drusus. The rejoicings were interrupted by terrible news. The legate of Germany, Quinctilius Varus, had been trapped in the forests of the interior and his entire army of three legions, XVII, XVIII and XIX—numbers henceforth regarded as ill-omened and never used again—had been wiped out by the German tribes, led by Arminius. Once again Augustus needed recruits, and found the response as bad as before. He was reduced to inflicting confiscation of property and *infamia* on citizens who refused to serve—or rather on every fifth man among those under thirty-five and on every tenth man among those over thirty-five. He later even inflicted the death penalty on some. It was perhaps on this occasion that he sold as a slave an *eques* who had cut off the thumbs of his two sons to disqualify them. He also recalled veterans to the colours, and enrolled freedmen.

Tiberius and Germanicus campaigned in Germany during the next two years, but rather with a view to re-establishing Roman prestige than to subduing the country again. The legions, by now eight in number, were withdrawn to the west bank of the Rhine, and any idea of the Elbe frontier was abandoned. On the North Sea coast the Frisians and the Chauci were perhaps retained under control, so that Augustus could still boast in the *Res Gestae* (26), 'I pacified the Gauls

76

and the Spains, and also Germany, where they are included by the Ocean from Gades to the mouth of the river Elbe'; one may suspect that an earlier version would have omitted 'the mouth of'.

Augustus was by now an old man, and he felt the disaster keenly. It is said that for many months he used from time to time to beat his head against a door and cry out, 'Quinctilius Varus, give me back my legions!' (Suetonius, *Augustus* 23, 2). Because of this one defeat, he completely abandoned the forward policy that he had hitherto pursued, and left among his written instructions to his successor that he should keep the Empire within its present boundaries.

In A.D. 13 Augustus' and Tiberius' powers were renewed for ten years by a consular law. No doubt in view of Augustus' age and declining health Tiberius was given full parity with him in the government of the provinces and the command of the armies, and also joint powers to conduct a census. As Tiberius probably did not possess the consular power in Italy which Augustus had enjoyed since 19 B.C. the second clause is understandable, but what power he lacked in the provinces is not clear. The census was held, and 4,937,000 citizens were counted, again a substantial rise.

When next year the census had been concluded Tiberius went north to take up the command in Illyricum. He had not gone far when he was recalled by the news that Augustus was seriously ill. He died on 19 August A.D. 14 at Nola. When he died the hope that he had expressed in 27 B.C. 'that the foundations of the commonwealth that I have laid will abide in their place', was fulfilled. Tiberius as his son was covered by the oath of allegiance, and it was promptly renewed to him by the consuls, the praetorian prefect, the prefect of the *annona*, the Senate, the armies and the people. Tiberius was already possessed of a consular *imperium* which covered directly or indirectly all the provinces and the armies, and they obeyed him without question. He had the tribunician power, in virtue of which he summoned the Senate, which voted divine honours to Augustus and the few prerogatives he lacked to himself.

6

The Constitutional Position

ACCORDING to Suetonius (*Augustus* 28) Augustus 'twice thought of restoring the Republic', first immediately after the defeat of Antonius, remembering that it had often been brought up against him that it was his responsibility that it had not been restored, and again from the depression caused by a long illness, when he actually summoned the magistrates and Senate to his house and handed over to them the accounts of the Empire. But reflecting that as a private citizen he would be in a dangerous position and that it would be risky to commit the state to the power of several persons, he persevered in keeping it in his own hands; whether the result or the motive was better may be doubted. He testified to this wish, which he often proclaimed, in an edict too, in the following words:

> May it be granted to me to establish the commonwealth on its foundations so safely and soundly, and to receive the reward for that action that I seek, that I may be called the author of the best state of things and when I die may carry with me the hope that the foundations of the commonwealth that I have laid will abide in their place (Suetonius, *Augustus* 28, 2).

The words of the edict have a certain ring of sincerity, and it may be that in 27 B.C. Augustus did envisage the possibility that at some future date, when he had secured the frontiers of the Empire, pacified the turbulent provinces, got the administration running smoothly, and brought about political harmony at home, he would be able to surrender his powers and leave the government to the magistrates and Senate, remaining only the venerated senior statesman whose advice would be sought on all important issues. If he had such a dream—and the edict for all its apparent sincerity may have been propaganda—the date for the restoration of the Republic continually receded, and eventually vanished from

78

sight. At no stage in his reign did he ever relax his hold on his great group of provinces and the legions which secured his power in the last resort; indeed after 23 B.C. he never returned a province to the Senate, but acquired many new ones, and never surrendered a legion but added several to his own total.

Another sign that he never seriously envisaged a genuine restoration of the Republic was his constant search for a successor, which began as early as 23 B.C., and concluded with the adoption of Tiberius in A.D. 4. Augustus could not, of course, designate his successor in constitutional law, for his powers were a number of grants made to him personally, some for his lifetime, others for a term of years. There were, however, some things that he could do to ensure the succession of a person of his own choice, or at least to favour his chances. He could bring him into his family, either by marrying him to his only daughter Julia, as he did with Marcellus, Agrippa and Tiberius in turn, or by adopting him as his son, as with Gaius and Lucius Caesar and Tiberius. The heir would thus share the prestige of the Julian house, and if adopted would be included under the oath of loyalty sworn to Augustus and his descendants in 33 B.C. Secondly the heir, if young—as they all were except Agrippa—could be given leave by the Senate to hold magistracies before the legal age, as were Marcellus, Tiberius, Drusus and Gaius and Lucius Caesar, and employed by Augustus as his legate for important wars and diplomatic missions. He thus gained political and military prestige of his own at an early age. Next he could, by vote of the Senate, receive the consular power for a term of years and share with Augustus the administration of his provinces and the conduct of frontier wars. Finally he could by vote of the Senate be accorded the tribunician power for a term of years. This last grant was more symbolic than practical, making the heir an equal colleague except for the consular power in Italy, and a few minor special prerogatives. A colleague in the consular *imperium* would, if Augustus died, be in a strong position, controlling the great bulk of the army for the remaining period of his term, but he would have no *locus standi* in Rome and Italy. The tribunician power would give him certain powers at Rome.

The risk of Augustus' death was covered by a colleague for the great part of his reign, from 23 B.C. to 12 B.C. by Agrippa (with the tribunician power from 18 B.C.), from 11 to 1 B.C. by Tiberius (with the tribunician power from 6 to 1 B.C.), from 1 B.C. to A.D. 4 by Gaius Caesar, and from A.D. 4 to 14 by Tiberius again (with tribunician power). It can be seen that Augustus was careful not to allow the possibility of an interregnum on his death.

He has been much criticized for seeking a successor from his own family only, instead of making a choice from the Senate as a whole. His choice was no doubt partly dictated by sentiment. He seems to have had a strong feeling for blood—he was deeply stricken by the death of his sister's son Marcellus, and doted on his grandsons Gaius and Lucius and was prostrated by their premature deaths. But there were also reasons of public policy for his choice. Augustus knew well from his own experience the devotion of the armies to Caesar's nearest relative and adoptive son, and this hereditary loyalty, now confirmed by the oath of 33 B.C., was likely to carry on to the next generation. If he designated as his successor a member of his own family and adopted him, the succession would run smoothly. If he designated an outsider, civil war would be likely.

The settlement of 27 B.C. was hailed by contemporary propaganda, and by the naïve and loyal Velleius, as the restoration of the Republic. Augustus himself was less explicit in his *Res Gestae* (34), merely claiming that 'I transferred the commonwealth from my own power to the free choice of the Senate and people'. He goes on to say that 'after that date I excelled all in authority but had no more power than my colleagues in the several magistracies'. The second half of the sentence is literally true. Augustus had technically an equal *imperium* with his colleagues in the consulship in 27–23 B.C. (and in 5 and 2 B.C.) In virtue of his *tribunicia potesta*s he might also be regarded as a colleague of the tribunes of the plebs from 23 B.C., and in virtue of his consular *imperium* of the successive pairs of consuls from 19 B.C. Here again his powers were equal. But as proconsul of more than half the Empire he was not strictly speaking a colleague of the proconsuls of the public provinces, over whom he exercised a *maius imperium*. And his colleagues in his provincial command, if they were, as they probably were, his equals constitutionally, were handpicked by himself.

His authority was ubiquitous and irresistible. The consuls and the other magistrates and promagistrates accepted his advice, and the Senate obediently passed the *senatus consulta* which he proposed. He began his social legislation with two plebiscites which he proposed himself in virtue of his tribunician power, but both the laws regulating manumission and the last law on marriage he got passed by the consuls. The *senatus consultum* of 4 B.C. establishing a new civil procedure for extortion is expressly attributed in the preamble to Augustus' initiative, but is moved by the consuls of the year. The series of *senatus consulta* establishing and regulating the new aqueduct commission are all moved by the consuls, though it is morally certain that Augustus conceived the whole scheme. Even in very minor matters Augustus' advice was sought and accepted. One Publius Paquius Scaeva, who had already been proconsul of Cyprus once, was reappointed *extra sortem* to regulate the state of the province 'by decree of the Senate by the authority of Augustus' (Ehrenberg and Jones, *Documents* 197). Augustus also sometimes used his authority rather than his *imperium maius* in the public provinces. In the first of his edicts about Cyrenaica (Ehrenberg and Jones, *Documents* 311, I) he uses very tactful language:

> Until the Senate considers the matter or I myself find a better solution, I think that future governors of the province of Crete and Cyrene will act well and properly, if they . . .

But even here he alludes clearly to his *imperium,* and in other edicts in the same series he uses the phrases 'it is my pleasure' or 'I command'.

Augustus' *imperium,* about which he is so coy in the *Res Gestae,* was in fact a far more important part of his powers than he admits. It was through his *imperium* that he controlled the greater part and eventually almost the whole of the army, that he governed his own group of provinces, which came to comprise about two-thirds of the Empire, and that he enforced his will, when he so wished, in the public provinces. He also used his *imperium* in Rome and Italy, commanding his praetorian guard, which he occasionally used for enforcing law and order in Italy; appointing a prefect of the city and furnishing him with the urban cohorts to enforce order in Rome; appointing a *praefectus vigilum* with seven cohorts of *vigiles* which had police as well as firefighting duties. He also, as we have seen, held censuses in virtue of his consular *imperium* and held conscriptions in Italy. Finally his extensive jurisdiction, both first instance and appellate, probably depended on his *imperium*.

Augustus' power was ultimately based neither on his constitutional prerogatives nor on his authority, but on the loyalty of the legions which he inherited from his adoptive father. At first he did his best to maintain their loyalty by leading them in war, but he was never very successful, and finally abandoned the active command of the armies after 26 B.C., henceforth employing his trusted colleague Agrippa or members of his own family as far as possible in important commands. Financially he was not over lavish to the troops. He did not raise their pay, which his adoptive father had doubled, and gave them only occasional triumphal donatives. He actually raised their minimum length of service from sixteen to twenty years, but he paid their discharge bounties in land or money regularly and promptly, and this probably counted for a lot. The absolute loyalty of the army was of paramount importance, but Augustus also enjoyed enthusiastic support from other groups. The events of 23–19 B.C. demonstrate emphatically that not only the urban populace of Rome, which pressed the dictatorship and perpetual consulate on him, but the middle class of Rome and Italy, which dominated the *comitia centuriata* and insisted on re-electing him consul, strongly supported his rule; the same class demonstrated their enthusiasm for him by flocking from all parts of Italy to Rome to elect him *pontifex maximus* in 12 B.C. As genuine, but politically of negligible importance, was the enthusiasm of the bulk of the provincials for the man who had brought them peace and better government.

These feelings of loyalty were given formal expression in the oath of loyalty which all Italy and the western provinces took in 33 B.C. and which, it would seem, the eastern provinces took after Actium, and the client kingdoms as they were annexed. How far the oath created loyalty may be doubted, but it probably reinforced existing sentiments.

If he enjoyed such widespread support, it may be asked why Augustus camouflaged his rule with Republican forms. The answer lies in the fate of his adoptive father, who enjoyed fully as much military and popular support, but was assassinated by a group of senators when he made it plain that he was never going to resign his dictatorship. There was an immensely strong sentiment among the upper classes, not only senators but *equites*, against absolute rule. They had been educated in the tradition of the annalists—the expulsion of the kings, the stern fathers of the Republic, the wise rule of the Senate—and the Republican form of government was sacrosanct to them. For the nobles, who had under the Republic competed for power and patronage, such sentiments were natural; but it would seem that they were widespread among the equestrian order too, despite their abstention from politics, especially among the men of property and education in the Italian towns. It is at any rate notable that the conspicuous Republican senators of the generations following Augustus were mostly men of equestrian family from Italian towns—men like Thrasea Paetus of Patavium and his son-in-law Helvidius Priscus. In Augustus' own time Livy, whom he mockingly called the Pompeian historian from his strongly Republican bias, was from Patavium, while Velleius Paterculus, who so highly praised both the old Republic and the new, came from a noble family of the Hirpini, who had become citizens and senators at the time of the Social wars.

The nobles cannot have regarded the restored Republic as anything but a fraudulent façade. But the vast majority of them reconciled themselves to it; under it they could without loss of self-respect compete for the old Republican magistracies and attain the consulship, even if it was now an empty honour, and hold two proconsulships, even if their provinces gave them no opportunity for triumphs or miltary glory, and perhaps less chance of financial gain. Senatorial plots against Augustus were few and feeble. After the serious conspiracy of Caepio and Murena in 23 B.C. there were no others of

83

importance. Egnatius Rufus after holding the aedileship in 21 B.C. and the praetorship in 20 illegally stood for the consulship in 19, and when his candidature was rejected, formed a plot against Augustus. One of Julia's lovers, Antonius Iullus, the triumvir's son, was accused of conspiracy in 2 B.C. and a grandson of Pompeius, Cornelius Cinna, was pardoned in A.D. 4. The rest were the work of very obscure persons.

Despite this Augustus seems to have distrusted the nobles to his dying day. He very rarely employed them as consular legates in command of his armies, preferring to entrust such posts either to members of his own family, such as Tiberius, Drusus and Gaius Caesar, or to men of humble origin who had risen by his patronage—Agrippa, Statilius Taurus, Sulpicius Quirinius, Marcus Lollius.

If the restored Republic was grudgingly accepted by the nobility, it seems to have been enthusiastically welcomed by the classes immediately below, the lesser senators who had no hopes of the consulship or of political power or influence, and the upper stratum of the equestrian order, which might aspire to the Senate. Velleius is a typical member of this stratum of society and his approval of the restored Republic is emphatic. This class was highly important to Augustus since it not only comprised many senators and potential senators, but also provided the vast majority of the commissioned officers in the army—nearly all the military tribunes of the legions, the prefects of *alae* and the tribunes of cohorts. The loyalty of all these officers was essential to Augustus' security, and a necessary condition of that loyalty was that the Republican constitution should be restored, at any rate in form. The men of this class had never had much chance of enjoying political power, and felt no loss if control was in fact exercised by one great statesman rather than contended for by rival factions, provided that the due procedure of the Republic was followed, the magistrates were elected by the people and performed their traditional functions, the Senate voted on *senatus consulta*, the people passed statutes, and the courts functioned according to law.

Augustus had many titles. From 12 B.C., when he was elected to the office, *pontifex maximus* usually comes first on inscriptions. Then comes consul, with the number of the last

consulship he had held (from 2 B.C. the figure is XIII), and
imperator, with the number of his salutations (which reached
XXI by the end of his life): since all the armies (except that
of the proconsul of Africa) were commanded by his legates
and fought under his auspices, their victories swelled the
total of Augustus' salutations. Either before or after *imperator* comes *tribunicia potestate* with a number—XXXVII
in A.D. 14: this was an important part of his titulature, never
omitted even in its most abbreviated form. Finally comes,
from A.D. 2, *pater patriae*.

None of these titles was suitable for everyday use, either in
speaking of him or addressing him. Augustus was extremely
nervous of any form of address which might suggest absolute
power. Once at the theatre the words 'O kind good master'
(*O dominum aequum et bonum*) occurred, and the audience
cheered him. He at once checked the applause, and the next
day issued an edict severely reproving them. He would
not even allow his children and grandchildren to call him
dominus, which was perfectly normal (Suetonius, *Augustus*
53).

The form of address which ultimately prevailed was
princeps. This does not mean *princeps senatus*, the senator
who was asked his opinion first—which Augustus was
from 27 B.C.—but is short for *princeps civitatis*. Under the
Republic leading statesmen had been called *principes civitatis;* now there was one *princeps* who overshadowed all the
rest. The title was admirably fitted to Augustus' policy; it
implied no powers, but only authority.

7

The Magistrates and the Senate

UNDER the restored Republic the consuls had very little to do except preside in the Senate, but the office retained its glamour, and was the gateway to the rich proconsulships of Africa and Asia, and for those of military ability to the command of armies. It was keenly contested between nobles, who had to keep up the family tradition, and new men, who aspired to make their families noble. At first the traditional pair of the good old days was strictly adhered to, but from about 5 B.C. the pressure became too great, and the annual number was doubled by a pair of suffect consuls.

The Sullan *lex annalis* laid down that no one could be a candidate for the consulship unless he had first been praetor, nor praetor until he had first been quaestor. Both these offices had also certain attractions of their own. The quaestorship gave admission to the Senate, the praetorship led on to a proconsulship and made a man eligible for a number of administrative posts. Both offices moreover had serious functions. About half the quaestors served in the provinces, and six served the two consuls and Augustus. The praetors still had the urban and peregrine jurisdiction, and the presidency of the *iudicia publica*, and two of them from 23 B.C. managed the *aerarium*. Moreover from 22 B.C. they took over from the aediles the attractive duty of giving the games. There was therefore adequate competition for these offices. There was, as far as we know, no particular pressure for the quaestorship with its twenty places, but the number of praetors was raised in 23 B.C. from eight to ten, and went up to twelve in the last years of the reign; in A.D. 11 the sixteen candidates were so persistent that Augustus allowed them all to hold office.

There was much less enthusiasm for the other offices of the traditional *cursus honorum*, which were not indispensable steps to the consulship, and had lost their old attractions. Under the new regime the tribunes of the plebs could not in practice propose popular legislation or bring the government to a standstill with their veto though they retained their powers in theory. They had in fact nothing to do, and a sufficient number of candidates sometimes failed to appear. In 13 B.C. owing to the lack of volunteers lots were drawn from all ex-quaestors under forty to fill the tribunate and in 12 B.C. Augustus ordered that each magistrate should pick an *eques* possessing the senatorial census, and that the people should elect from them; these *equites* had the option of becoming senators or remaining in their old station after their year of office. Again in A.D. 12 *equites* were allowed to stand for the tribunate.

The aediles also lost in the course of the reign their more important functions—the control of the corn supply in 22 B.C., the aqueducts in 11 B.C., the fire service in A.D. 6. Even worse from the point of view of candidates, in 22 B.C. they lost the management of the games and the chance of winning popularity for the next hurdle, the praetorian elections. All they had left was the repair of the streets and a petty jurisdiction in commercial cases. It is not surprising that in A.D. 5 and in many other years, according to Dio, the aedile-ship was filled compulsorily by lot from ex-quaestors and ex-tribunes.

The vigintivirate, the group of minor offices held before the quaestorship, also caused trouble. Paquius Scaeva, who omitted it and proceeded directly to his quaestorship, was ordered by decree of the Senate to hold the decemvirate *stlitibus iudicandis* next year and serve as *quattuorvir capitalis* the year after that; warned by this experience he dutifully held both a tribunate of the plebs and an aedileship and the post of *iudex quaestionis* before aspiring to the praetorship. In 13 B.C. the Senate authorized *equites* to hold these offices, without any implied obligation to proceed to the quaestorship. Eventually, before A.D. 20, the vigintivirate was made a compulsory step to the quaestorship, and at some date the rule was made that all senators except patricians must hold either the tribunate of the plebs or the aedileship before becoming praetors.

It is obvious that the elections for the lower offices (except perhaps the quaestorship) cannot have been very exciting. It was very different with the elections for the praetors and consuls held in the *comitia centuriata*. Corruption was rife. In 18 B.C. Augustus had to enact a *lex Iulia de ambitu*, which debarred candidates who were guilty of electoral corruption from office for five years. In 8 B.C. he demanded from all candidates a deposit, which they would forfeit if guilty of bribery. He used moreover normally to give the members of his own two tribes, Seaptia and Fabia, 1000 sesterces a head, in the hope that they might thus be less likely to take bribes from others. The elections were also sometimes disorderly even at the end of the reign. In A.D. 7 Augustus had to nominate all the magistrates owing to the prolonged electoral riots.

In A.D. 5 the consuls, Lucius Valerius Messalla Volesus and Gnaeus Cornelius Cinna Magnus, passed a law, doubtless inspired by Augustus, to reform the procedure in the *comitia centuriata* for the election of praetors and consuls. Ten new centuries were formed in memory of Gaius and Lucius Caesar, consisting exclusively of senators and of *equites* of the three judicial decuries; they were allocated by tribes to the centuries by lot at the actual moment of voting. The ten centuries voted first, and 'destined' twelve praetors and two consuls. Then followed the voting of the centuriate assembly. Candidates rejected by the centuries of Gaius and Lucius Caesar were not apparently excluded from competition, but the preliminary vote of these ten very select centuries must have given a great advantage, even greater than the vote of the old *centuria praerogativa*, to the men they selected. The effect of this procedure on the elections is disputable, but it would appear that from 18 B.C. to A.D. 4 the nobles had kept the consulate to themselves, and that after A.D. 4 more new men were successful. This would be the natural result of a procedure which gave decisive influence to ten centuries comprising 600 senators and 3000 *equites*.

Augustus had one constitutional power in connection with the elections. Like the consuls he could—presumably in virtue of his consular power—receive (or reject) candidatures (*professiones*) for the consulship and praetorship, or as was sometimes said, nominate (*nominare*) to these offices. Augustus' list of candidates naturally had some prestige, but the consuls could also nominate, and there was no question of Augustus refusing *professiones* except for weighty reasons.

Apart from this Augustus could and did canvass for candidates whom he specially favoured; Suetonius says that he used to go round the tribes with his own candidates and beg them for their votes in the customary way. All prominent statesmen did this, but Augustus' 'commendation' naturally carried most weight. He went on doing this until A.D. 8, when owing to growing infirmity he gave up a personal canvass, and posted up a list of the candidates whom he favoured, urging the people to vote for them. The election of such candidates seems by the end of the reign to have become automatic—their names were perhaps put to the vote separately before the rest, in which case they could hardly fail. By the end of the reign it had also become a convention that Augustus should 'commend' four out of the twelve praetors. Commendation was hardly necessary for the lower offices, when competition was so slight, and to judge by Tiberius' practice Augustus does not seem to have commended to the consulate.

Augustus arranged that the decurions of his twenty-eight Italian colonies should record their votes in advance for the Roman elections in their home towns, and send them up to Rome for the election day sealed. This was not, it would seem, a move to make the voting at the Roman elections more representative of the whole of Italy, but was designed to enhance the status of his colonies—and perhaps to secure 2800 votes for his candidates.

While the old Republican magistracies tended to become sinecures, senators were not deprived of opportunities for useful if not very exciting administrative work. Indeed Suetonius (*Augustus* 37) says that Augustus,

> In order that a larger number should have a part in the administration of the state, thought up new offices, the curatorships of the public works, of the aqueducts, of the bed of the Tiber, the distribution of corn to the people, the prefecture of the city, a commission of three for revising the roll of the Senate and another for revising the squadrons of *equites* whenever there was need.

Augustus did not, of course, invent offices to give senators jobs, but as far as possible he avoided taking over departments of the administration of Rome himself, and entrusted them to senatorial commissioners. The aediles, for instance, were very inefficient at controlling fires. Augustus first provided them with a fire brigade of 600 public slaves in 22 B.C. He next in 7 B.C. distributed the control of the fire service, dividing the city into fourteen regions, for which the aediles, tribunes and praetors—twenty-eight magistrates in all—drew lots annually. It was not until A.D. 6 that he took over the service from the Senate and placed it under an equestrian prefect of his own. Again the aediles often failed to maintain the supply of corn. In 22 B.C. after a crisis Augustus arranged for two prefects of praetorian rank to be elected annually by the Senate to distribute the corn, and four years later raised their number to four of higher seniority to be chosen annually by lot. In a later crisis he had three consulars appointed in 7 and 6 B.C. It was not till the end of the reign that he took over the service and appointed an equestrian *praefectus annonae*.

Another function taken from the aediles was the care of the aqueducts, which was handed over in 11 B.C. to a commission of three senators, a consular, a praetorian and a junior member of the house. They were elected by the Senate on the nomination of Augustus, and had apparently no fixed term of office; Messalla Corvinus, the first consular curator, served from 11 B.C. to A.D. 13. An inscription records a *curator aedium sacrarum monumentorumque publicorum tuendorum*, showing that the repair of public buildings had passed from the aediles to a commission of senators. Another inscription records a commission of five senators headed by a consular, *curatores locorum publicorum iudicandorum*. Other new offices included the curators of the Italian roads, created in 20 B.C.; they were of praetorian rank. In A.D. 6 the new military treasury was put under three praetorian *praefecti*, chosen by lot for three years. Besides the two occasional triumvirates mentioned by Suetonius, a commission of three consulars was appointed in A.D. 6 to review and reduce expenditure.

The main advantage of these new quasi-magistracies was that their duties were more specifically defined than those of the old magistrates, and were much more limited. They were also assigned to more senior men, praetorians or even consulars. In some cases too their tenure was longer. In the method of appointment Augustus wavered between election by the Senate and by lot. Election would seem more rational, but in the case of the *praefecti aerarii* (*Saturni*) Augustus found that it led to electoral corruption, and substituted for them two extra praetors, making the treasury two of the *provinciae* for which the praetors drew lots.

The three revisions of the senatorial roll which Augustus himself conducted, despite the odium involved, in 28 B.C., 18 B.C. and 11 B.C., and the fourth which he entrusted to a commission in A.D. 4, show what importance he attached to the respectability of the Senate. Apart from these occasional purges he took one other step to raise its tone. Under the Republic there had been no official property qualification, though the expenses of a senatorial career were high. Augustus laid down a qualification and apparently raised it from time to time. According to Suetonius the figure was first 800,000 sesterces, then 1,200,000. According to Dio it was first, in 18 B.C., fixed at the equestrian census, 400,000, but had risen before 13 B.C. to 1,000,000, and in A.D. 4 he speaks of 1,200,000 as the figure. At the beginning of Tiberius' reign, however, it was a million. The data could be combined as a progression from 400,000 to 800,000 and 1,000,000 and 1,200,000, and a final reduction to a million. The figures are considerable, but there were large numbers of prosperous Italian families that possessed as much. Some senators and potential senators were excluded, but they were mostly nobles impoverished in the civil wars, and Augustus made up the census of such as he deemed deserving.

More doubtful is the *latus clavus*. In the later Empire senators' sons wore the tunic with the broad purple stripe which was the privilege of senators as soon as they came of age, and could stand for the quaestorship and thus enter the Senate without imperial permission. Commoners on the other hand had to obtain from the emperor the grant of the *latus clavus* before they could stand. In the late Republic and in the early part of Augustus' reign not only senators' sons but any aspirant to the Senate put on the *latus clavus*—Ovid, of equestrian rank, did so about 23 B.C. without imperial permission, and became a *vigintivir*, and only then, when he decided not to stand for the quaestorship, took the narrow stripe of the *eques*. Augustus is said to have formally permitted sons of senators to wear the broad stripe and attend the Senate. He thereby encouraged the hereditary tendency which the Senate had always had, and implicitly discouraged outsiders to stand. Whether he went so far as to exclude them from candidature except by his express permission is doubtful.

The old nobility, in so far as it survived, took a leading part in the Augustan Senate, and no doubt other old senatorial families of less renown retained their places. But there was plenty of room for newcomers, particularly as the old families tended to die out. According to Claudius, 'My uncles the deified Augustus and Tiberius Caesar wished all the flower of the colonies and municipalities everywhere [in Italy], honest wealthy men, to be members of this house' (Dessau, *Inscriptiones Latinae Selectae* 212). We know of some examples. The people of Superaegum proudly boasted that Quintus Varius Geminus 'was the first of all the Paeligni to be made a senator and to hold these honours'; he only achieved a praetorship and a proconsulate and was legate of Augustus twice. Another Paelignian, Ovid, might have beaten Varius in the race, but that he withdrew from it. A third, C. Pontius Paelignus, later got as far as the aedileship.

To enhance the dignity of sessions, Augustus ruled that all senators must before taking their seats make an offering of wine and incense on the altar of the temple in which the session was held. Meetings were not always dignified; Augustus was sometimes heckled by cries of 'I don't understand', or 'I would contradict you if I had an opportunity of speaking', and when he walked out in indignation was sometimes pursued with protests, 'senators ought to be allowed to speak on public affairs' (Suetonius, *Augustus* 54). In general however it would seem that sessions of the Senate were quiet, not to say dull. In the first place Augustus seems rarely to have consulted the house on important issues. Dio indeed says that he often invited senators to send in their comments in writing beforehand, but he is only recorded to have done this once, about the revenue of the new military treasury in A.D. 6, and on that occasion he ignored all suggestions and insisted on his own proposal. Seven years later he allowed a free debate in the Senate on this very controversial topic—the five per cent duty on inheritances was bitterly resented by senators—but frightened the house into confirming the tax by making ostentatious preparations for levying the property tax (*tributum*), which had last been imposed on Roman citizens in 167 B.C. In the second place he set up a drafting committee of the Senate consisting of himself, the consuls, one from each college of magistrates, and fifteen other senators chosen by lot, changing every six months. It is seen functioning in the *senatus consultum* of 4 B.C. on trials for extortion:

> Whereas the consuls Gaius Calvisius Sabinus and Lucius Passienus Rufus spoke on the matters which Imperator Caesar Augustus, our *princeps*, with the advice of the committee which he has by lot from the Senate, wished to be brought before the Senate by us, bearing on the security of the allies of the Roman people, it was resolved by the Senate. . . . (Ehrenberg and Jones, *Documents* 311, V).

This preparatory committee was fully representative of the Senate and no doubt expedited business, but it must have tended to reduce the full Senate to a rubber stamp. In A.D. 13, when he had become too infirm to attend the Senate, Augustus procured a *senatus consultum* whereby the drafting committee was enlarged to himself and Tiberius and his two adoptive grandsons, the consuls and the consuls designate, and twenty senators chosen by lot annually. This committee was empowered to enact measures which had the force of *senatus consulta*. Such an arrangement was clearly a temporary expedient, and the whole idea of a drafting committee was promptly dropped by Tiberius.

If sessions of the Senate were largely occupied with formally passing predigested measures, it is not surprising that attendance was poor. Augustus had twice to increase the fines on absentees, in 17 and 9 B.C. He also in 9 B.C. reduced sessions to two per month, on the Kalends and the Ides, and reduced the quorum, already lowered from 400 in 11 B.C., laying down different figures for various kinds of business; if there was not a quorum the measure was registered as a *senatus auctoritas*. Finally in September and October only as many senators, chosen by lot, as sufficed to make a quorum, were obliged to attend.

8

The Provinces

WHEREAS the divine providence that guides our life has displayed its zeal and benevolence by ordaining for our life the most perfect good, bringing to us Augustus, whom it has filled with virtue for the benefit of mankind, employing him as a saviour for us and our descendants, him who has put an end to wars and adorned peace; and Caesar being made manifest to us has exceeded the hopes of all who before brought good tidings, not only outstripping all benefactors before him, but leaving no hope to those who shall come after to surpass him; and the birthday of the god is the beginning of all the good tidings brought by him to the world. . . . (Ehrenberg and Jones, *Documents* 98).

The messianic language of this decree of the province of Asia passed in 9 B.C. is unusual, but the same sentiments are voiced in more prosaic terms by scores of provincial inscriptions. Nor is there any reason to doubt their sincerity, for the vast outburst of civic building in Augustus' reign testifies to a great increase in the prosperity of the governing class in the provincial cities, from whose surplus wealth the cost of civic buildings was mostly met.

One of the principal reasons for the gratitude of the provincials and their prosperity was that Augustus finally brought to an end the succession of civil wars which had since Caesar crossed the Rubicon afflicted the provinces with billeting of trops, requisition of supplies and financial extortion, apart from the devastation of war. Augustus, it is true, waged wars for nearly all his reign, but his wars were either beyond the frontiers of the Empire or in remote provinces like northwestern Spain or Dalmatia and Pannonia. These areas suffered severely; asked by Tiberius why they had revolted, Bato, one of the Pannonian leaders, replied: 'The fault is yours; you send to guard your flocks not shepherds and dogs but wolves' (Cassius Dio LVI, 16). The great bulk of the provinces, however, including all the richest, were after 30 B.C. spared the exactions of war.

In the second place Augustus, as will be argued in the next section, seems to have substituted for the various systems of taxation hitherto prevailing in the provinces a more equitable and more or less uniform scheme. It is unlikely that the rate was lower, but the burden was more fairly distributed, and, what was most important, the tax contractors, whose exorbitant profits had enormously increased the burden, were eliminated.

A minor but useful reform was the allocation of fixed salaries to provincial governors. Under the Republic governors had received annual grants (*annuus sumptus*) from the Senate to cover all their expenses—pay for their troops, the cost of requisitioned supplies and so forth, including the expense accounts (*salaria*) of their legates, quaestors, prefects, tribunes and other members of their staff. It would not appear that they could claim *salaria* for themselves, but as the *annuus sumptus* was generous, it was not difficult to manipulate the accounts so as to make a good profit. The salaries given to governors under the new regime were very large; in the early third century the proconsul of Asia got a million sesterces for his year, and as salaries were very stable in the first two centuries of the principate, it may well be that Augustus fixed this figure. Even so it probably represented a saving as against the proconsul's earlier rake-off. A minor reform coupled with the grant of regular salaries was the provision of travel allowances instead of the mules and tents supplied under the Republic.

Augustus made another minor but useful reform which improved the provincial administration, the institution of a public post to facilitate communication between them and Rome. No such thing existed under the Republic, and governors were thus almost cut off from the Senate. Cicero as proconsul of Cilicia sent two despatches in his year to Rome, and for his private correspondence made use of the messenger system of the tax contracting companies. Augustus at first stationed runners at intervals along the main roads, who passed letters from hand to hand. This must have been slow, and he later stationed carriages and teams along the roads so that one messenger could carry his letter the whole way with relays of transport. This had the additional advantage that he could carry verbal messages as well and explain and expand the letter. It is not known who furnished the carriages and teams under Augustus, but later it was the cities on the route, and they found it a heavy burden.

Augustus probably initiated the practice, prevalent in the next reign, of trying cases of extortion not before the regular public court, which was very corrupt, but before the Senate. Senators were by no means incorruptible, and were too prone to be lenient to fellow senators, but if Augustus presided at the session or even only attended, he could secure a severe verdict by his authority. He also invented a new and simplified procedure whereby provincials could, if they did not wish to bring a capital charge, sue a governor for simple restitution at much less expense. The procedure was that the complainants approached any magistrate who had the right of convening the Senate—a consul, praetor or tribune—and he as soon as possible convened the Senate and appointed a senator of their choice as their advocate, and drew by lot four consulars, three praetorians and two other senators, who were reduced by alternate rejections of the accused and the accusers to five. These five decided on the charges and fixed the damages within thirty days. The accuser was allowed to subpoena five or ten witnesses, according to whether he was acting for himself or for his city, but only from Italy, as the chief expense and hardship of a regular trial was the bringing of witnesses from the provinces to Rome and their maintenance for a lengthy period while the trial was pending and pursuing its leisurely course.

The formation of provincial *concilia* to conduct the worship of Rome and Augustus also made for more effective prosecutions for extortion. The primary function of the *concilium* was to elect a provincial high priest and celebrate sacrifices and games, but it was natural that a body consisting of delegates from all the cities of a province should discuss matters of common interest, and if they had serious complaints against their ex-governor organize and pay for a prosecution jointly. In the next reign there are recorded cases of a joint prosecution by a province.

THE PROVINCES

Augustus could also use his authority or *maius imperium* to reform scandalous abuses which came to his notice. In 6 B.C. he did so in Cyrenaica. This province had criminal courts of the Roman type, manned by the resident Roman citizens, who were a small and poor community—there were only 215 persons assessed at 2500 denarii or over, which was the qualification for jury service. They had formed conspiracies, one accusing, others giving evidence, others sitting on the juries, to convict the Greeks of imaginary crimes—or more commonly no doubt to extract blackmail by the threat of prosecution. Augustus ordered that if possible the qualification for jury service should be raised to 7500 denarii, or at least 3750, and that, if a Greek accused asked for it, the jury should be half Romans and half Greeks of the same property qualification. He also advised the governor not to accept a Roman as accuser in a murder case where the victim was a Greek. He also ruled that in civil cases between Greeks, the governor should appoint a Greek judge, from a city other than that or those of the litigants.

By the end of Augustus' reign there were a considerable number of Roman colonies and municipalities and Latin communities in some of the provinces. This was a recent development. Under the Republic there had been one important Roman colony, Narbo, in Gaul, and perhaps three or four lesser settlements in Corsica and Africa; no *municipia*; and one solitary Latin town, Carteia in Spain. The movement had been begun in a big way by Caesar, who during his dictatorship planted large numbers of colonies of veterans, mostly in the western provinces, created it would seem a substantial number of *municipia* in the same areas, and gave Latin rights to all the cities of Sicily, and probably to a large number in Gallia Narbonensis and Spain. The movement, particularly the foundation of colonies, continued under the triumvirate and under Augustus. By his reign there were— the numbers are all liable to revision—twenty-five colonies and as many municipalities and close on fifty Latin towns in the three Spanish provinces, about twenty per cent of the total number of communities. In Gallia Narbonensis there were eight colonies and twenty-seven Latin towns; the barbarous Gallia Comata on the other hand had only one colony,

Lugdunum. In Africa there were six colonies and fifteen *municipia* and one Latin city (out of 516 in all), in Sicily five colonies, two *municipia* and three Latin cities (out of sixty-six). In the Greek speaking provinces it was apparently considered inappropriate to give Roman and Latin status to the local communities; some degree of Romanization was it seems a necessary prerequisite. At any rate there was only one *municipium* (Stobi, on the northern frontier of Macedonia) and no Latin towns in the East. Nine colonies were planted in Macedonia and Achaea and six in Galatia, but elsewhere colonies also were rare, two each in Bithynia-Pontus and in Asia, one in Syria and one in Crete.

The planting of a colony of veterans was not an unmixed blessing to the city concerned. The land required was normally, it would seem, land which had been confiscated for rebellion, though some was purchased. The settlers henceforth formed the citizen body, and the old inhabitants might either become a separate community or become subjects of the colony. Pausanias remarks that Augustus highly favoured the Achaean city of Patrae, and gave the old citizens the status of colonists when he planted his veterans there. This seems from Pausanias' language to be an exceptional case.

The grant of municipal status was a very different matter. In these cases the native citizens all received the Roman citizenship and the town was given a constitution on the model of an Italian town. Latin status was a lesser privilege. The natives became Latins, that is became subject to Roman law, and the town received a constitution on the Italian model. Furthermore the annual magistrates received Roman citizenship on retirement. This meant that in process of time the upper classes became Romans.

Latin towns were according to Strabo not subject to the orders of the governor. He must have had jurisdiction, but presumably the city was free from interference in its internal affairs. Roman colonies and *municipia* must obviously have been equally privileged. Roman colonists paid no land tax but enjoyed what was called the *ius Italicum*; their land, that is, was legally assimilated to the tax free soil of Italy. It would have been inequitable to make veterans pay tax if planted in a provincial colony, but enjoy immunity if they were lucky enough to be settled in Italy. On the other hand *municipia* normally continued to pay tribute, and so did Latin towns. It would have been financially ruinous to reduce the taxation of Spain by twenty per cent. The total result was thus that in the older and more civilized provinces of the West a certain number of provincial communities were spared the arbitrary intervention of the governor, and their citizens, or the upper stratum of their citizens, were protected against his arbitrary justice by *appellatio ad Caesarem*.

How far the standards of conduct improved among provincial governors it is impossible to say. There was, it is true, a higher probability of conviction if they were brought to trial, which may have deterred some, but there is no reason to believe that the character of the Roman nobility changed suddenly for the better after 27 B.C. They were still grossly extravagant and looked to their provinces to pay their debts and re-establish their fortunes. The civil war had not made them any less brutal. Seneca (*On Anger* II, 5, 5) tells a grim anecdote of the blueblooded Valerius Messalla Volesus, proconsul of Asia about A.D. 12, who, having executed 300 persons in one day, exclaimed (in Greek), as he walked proudly among the corpses: 'What a royal deed!' Volesus was in fact condemned by the Senate. Under Tiberius eight provincial governors were prosecuted, and nearly all condemned. Of these five were proconsuls, and three legates of Augustus; which does not suggest that the standard of government was markedly higher in the imperial provinces.

Apart from such general measures and occasional interventions, Augustus left the government of the public provinces unchanged, so anxious was he to restore the old Republican system. Proconsuls, and their legates and quaestors, had a strictly annual tenure, despite the obvious disadvantages of so quick a turnover, and ex-consuls, ex-praetors and quaestors continued to draw their provinces by lot without regard to their ability or character; legates were as under the Republic chosen by their proconsuls, ex-consuls having three, ex-praetors only one. Augustus could of course use his authority in the Senate to get a man of experience whom he recommended appointed to a province outside the lot, as in the case of Paquius Scaeva, who was voted a second proconsulship of Cyprus 'to settle the status of the province of Cyprus for the future' (Ehrenberg and Jones, *Documents* 197); but it was only in exceptional circumstances that he broke the routine in this way. Former consuls and praetors drew for their provinces at least five years after holding office according to the *lex Pompeia* of 52 B.C. and by the end of the reign the interval was actually much longer. When from about 5 B.C. it became normal for two pairs of consuls to be elected each year, a queue inevitably began to form for the two consular provinces of Asia and Africa, and similarly when the number of praetors rose in A.D. 11 to twelve, and the praetorian provinces sank in the latter part of the reign to eight.

Strabo gives a complete list of the public provinces, but excuses himself from doing the same for Caesar's provinces, on the ground that their administration was fluid, and that they were grouped in different ways at different times as Augustus wished. Strictly speaking it might be said that all the parts of the Empire which he ruled were his *provincia* and that what were called his provinces were merely portions of it which he allocated to his several legates. Be that as it may, a fairly stable administrative structure had come into being by the end of the reign. The system of *legati Augusti pro praetore* was an extension of the Republican system, under which every proconsul had one or more legates to assist him; in the extraordinary commands of the late Republic the number of *legati* had been considerable. What was rather novel was that a proconsul should not go to his province at all, but divide it between his legates; but Pompey as proconsul of the Spains had done this before. Augustus, like other proconsuls, chose his own *legati,* assigned them to what tasks he thought fit, and employed them as long as he liked. Their term of office was usually longer than a year—three years eventually became the norm—and might be very prolonged. Legates might be ex-consuls or ex-praetors. Ex-consuls governed provinces of military importance with two or more legions, ex-praetors lesser provinces with only one legion or none.

A few of Caesar's provinces were governed by equestrian officers, usually with the title of prefect. These prefects no doubt derived from the *praefecti* whom Republican proconsuls had on their staff and employed, usually on a temporary basis, to command bodies of auxiliary troops or govern towns or small districts. If so Augustus' first prefect was a portentous expansion of its Republican model. When he annexed the kingdom of Egypt in 30 B.C. he appointed as its first governor an equestrian officer—in fact a personal friend, Cornelius Gallus, the poet—with the title of prefect. At the same time he assigned to Egypt a very large garrison, three legions, three *alae* and nine cohorts, which Gallus commanded. It naturally followed from this that the prefect's subordinate officers were also of equestrian rank. The legions were commanded by prefects and not senatorial *legati*. The *iuridicus* and the other civilian assistants of the prefect were likewise *equites*. Strangest of all a strict rule was laid down that no senator might visit the country without his express consent. The reason for this strange anomaly is given by Tacitus, 'for fear that Italy might be starved out by whoever held that province, whose frontiers by sea and by land could be held against huge armies by however small a garrison', in other words that Egypt was at the same time so vital to the corn supply of Rome, and so strategically defensible, that it was unsafe to allow a senator, a potential rival, to obtain control of it. Elsewhere Tacitus explains the peculiar position of Egypt as due to the fact that 'the province was difficult of access, rich in grain, excitable and turbulent owing to its superstition and irresponsibility, ignorant of laws and unacquainted with magistrates'. The last part of this dictum hardly explains an equestrian prefect, but accounts for the large garrison. It was evidently anticipated that the Egyptians might be troublesome, but in fact they proved quite passive, and one legion was withdrawn before the end of the reign.

Tacitus says that Augustus, 'set Egypt apart', or 'kept it within his household'. These figurative phrases have been taken very literally by some, who have described Egypt as the personal estate of the emperor. As far as official language went this was not so. The royal land became the public land, the royal banks the public banks, only the ancient Pharaonic title 'royal scribe' survived. Augustus claimed in the *Res Gestae* (27), 'I added Egypt to the empire of the Roman people' and even Tacitus called Egypt a province. Nor was this merely a matter of official terminology.

The revenues of Egypt according to Velleius Paterculus flowed into the public treasury of the Roman people, the *aerarium*.

The arrangement was, however, constitutionally very irregular, and Octavian (as he then was), when he got back to Rome, had a law passed conferring upon the prefect of Egypt an *imperium* like that of a proconsul.

Egypt was anomalous in another way. Nearly all the other provinces were agglomerations of self-governing communities, cities in the more civilized areas, tribes in the barbarous north and west, and these communities not only managed their local affairs, but under the Augustan system collected the imperial taxes. The provincial governor was left only military and judicial functions, apart from general supervision of the local administration. In Egypt there were only three cities, the old Greek colony of Naucratis, Ptolemais, founded by Ptolemy I in the Thebaid, and Alexandria. The first two were small and harmless, and were left to govern themselves. Alexandria was a huge city of over 300,000 free inhabitants, apart from slaves. Its population was very mixed, comprising large numbers of Egyptians, Jews and other foreigners besides the Greek citizens, and it was as a result prone to disorders. The later Ptolemies had thought it wise to deprive it of its council and make it subject to royal officers, and Octavian refused a petition from the city for the restoration of the council and maintained its existing status.

The rest of the country was administered by an intricate and highly centralized bureaucracy. It was divided into about forty administrative districts called nomes, each governed by a *strategus*, assisted by a 'royal scribe' and half a dozen other officials. Everything, down to the appointment of a village clerk, was managed by the central ministries in Alexandria. Octavian decided to take over the whole intricate machine as it stood, appointing a handful of Roman officials to control it. The prefect was assisted at Alexandria by a judicial assessor (*iuridicus*) and two financial officials, both bearing Ptolemaic titles, the 'manager' (*ad dioecesin*) and the 'special account' (*idiologus*): the former dealt with regular revenue, the latter with fines and confiscations. He also appointed three officials to supervise the three main districts (*epistrategiae*),

THE PROVINCES

the Thebaid, the Seven Nomes and the Lower Country, into
which he divided the country.

Augustus later created other equestrian provinces, but they
were all of minor importance. The Maritime and the Cottian
Alps, Raetia and Noricum were difficult mountainous districts inhabited by unruly tribes. They needed a military
governor on the spot, but were too small for a senatorial
legate. Another such province was Moesia and Trebellia until
it became large enough to require a legate. Cyprus, before it
became a public province in 23 B.C., and Sardinia, after it
was handed on to Augustus in A.D. 6, were also governed by
equestrian officers, but with the title of acting legate (*pro
legato*). It was perhaps felt that the old provinces ought not
to be degraded to prefectures; the *equites* who governed them
were supposed to be deputizing for senatorial legates.

The last equestrian province to be created during Augustus' reign was of a rather different type, nearer to Egypt
than the rest. The Jews and Samaritans were, it is true, a
turbulent people, addicted to riots, brigandage and even
rebellion, and the prefect of Judaea had some auxiliary
troops, mainly the old royal army. But its administration was
organized on the same lines as Egypt. The system can be
traced back to the Hasmonaean kings and probably dates to
the third century B.C. when Palestine was a Ptolemaic province. There were two cities only, Caesarea and Sebaste, and
the rest of the country was divided into districts called top-
archies, and each village had its clerk, appointed by the
central government.

Strabo describes the early arrangements in Spain in some
detail. In the south there was the public province of Baetica,
with its proconsul and his legate and quaestor. The rest of
the peninsula was divided into a small province, Lusitania,
in the southwest and the large province of Hither Spain or
Tarraconensis, covering all the north and east. Lusitania,
which had no legion, was governed by a *legatus Augusti pro
praetore*, of praetorian rank, assisted by a junior *legatus
Augusti*. This is contrary to the rule which later prevailed
that unarmed imperial provinces, and those with one legion
only, were governed by one praetorian legate unaided. In
Tarraconensis, which had three legions, the *legatus Augusti*

pro praetore was of consular rank, and had three junior *legati*. One of these commanded two legions and administered Callaecia and the country of the Astures, the second had one legion and governed all the northern coastal area from the territory of the Cantabri to the Pyrenees, the third administered the pacified and civilized area of the Ebro valley. The consular spent his winters at Tarraco or New Carthage administering justice and his summers in touring the whole province and inspecting his *legati* and their legions. This arrangement again differs from what later prevailed. A consular legate normally—the only exceptions are Spain and Britain—had no administrative or judicial assistant, but only a legate for each of his legions, and a legate is never found commanding two legions.

Augustus thus became as his reign went on rather parsimonious in staffing his provinces. Whereas the praetorian proconsul of a public province, who had no military responsibilities, had a *legatus pro praetore* to assist him in his judicial and administrative duties, a praetorian *legatus Augusti pro praetore* had no assistant, even if he had to command a legion. Similarly a consular proconsul had three legates, one of whom presumably commanded the legion in Africa, but the others were civilian assistants. A consular legate of Augustus had only a legate for each legion, and no civilian assistants. Proconsuls also had quaestors which legates of Augustus lacked; Augustus had only two quaestors as proconsul, and could not afford them for his legates. This was less of a burden on legates of Augustus as his procurators did all their financial work, but in the public provinces quaestors often helped in judicial business.

Moving eastward Gallia Narbonensis was after 23 B.C. a public province. Gallia Comata seems often to have formed one province, as when it was under the command of Tiberius or Drusus, but was eventually split into three unarmed provinces under *legati Augusti pro praetore* of praetorian rank. In the southwest was Aquitania, which comprised several Celtic tribes in addition to the Aquitani; in the northeast Belgica, where again some Celtic tribes were added to the Belgae; between them Lugdunensis, so called from the colony of Lugdunum which Munatius Plancus had founded in

43 B.C., comprising the bulk of the Celtic tribes. The eight
legions of Gaul were towards the end of the reign concentrated along the Rhine, and formed into two divisions of four
legions each commanded by consular legates who also administered the tribes along the left bank of the Rhine. Moving
eastwards again the four Alpine districts were governed by
equestrian prefects—the Maritime Alps, the Cottian Alps,
Raetia and Noricum. These provinces had no legions, despite the fact that the two last extended to the upper Danube
and thus had a frontier with the free Germans. Next came
Illyricum, Pannonia and Moesia, all three important military provinces, Pannonia with three legions and Illyricum
and Moesia with two legions each at the end of the reign,
and governed by consular legates. Illyricum had been in the
earlier part of the reign a public province, and was handed
over to Augustus in 11 B.C. The other two had been imperial
from their annexation. To the south of them were the public
provinces of Macedonia and Achaea and the kingdom of
Thrace. Returning to the western Mediterranean, Sicily was
a public province governed by a praetorian proconsul. Sardinia had the same status until A.D. 6 when it was handed
over to Augustus and put under an equestrian *pro legato*.
In Africa, Mauretania was a kingdom, ruled by King Juba
(25 B.C.–A.D. 23). Next came the public province of Africa
(including Numidia), whose consular proconsul still commanded a legion, and next Cyrenaica, which was joined to
Crete to form a public province whose proconsul was of
praetorian rank. Next came Egypt, whose peculiar administrative system has already been described; it had three legions
at the beginning of the reign, reduced to two at its end.

In Asia Minor there were two public provinces. Asia was
large and wealthy, and governed by a consular proconsul,
Bithynia-Pontus was much reduced in its Pontic half from
Pompeius' great province by sundry grants of cities to kings
and dynasts, and was governed by a praetorian proconsul. To
the south of Asia was the free federation of Lycian cities,
to the east the amorphous imperial province of Galatia. As
annexed on Amyntas' death in 25 B.C. it consisted of Galatia
proper, the territories of three Gallic tribes, Pisidia, Lycaonia
and Pamphylia, subsequently (in 5 and 2 B.C.) parts of

AUGUSTUS

Paphlagonia and Pontus were added to it on the death of their dynasts. Parts of the province, notably Pisidia, were turbulent —Amyntas had been killed in tribal warfare against the Homonadeis—and at first Galatia had a *legatus Augusti pro praetore* of consular rank, presumably with two legions. Some time after 12 B.C., when he held the consulship, Pisidia was pacified by Sulpicius Quirinius and five veteran colonies were planted in the area. Subsequently Galatia lost its legions and its legate became praetorian. The eastern part of Asia was occupied by two kingdoms, Pontus under Polemo (36–8 B.C.), succeeded by his widow Pythodoris, and Cappadocia with Armenia Minor and Cilicia Tracheia under Archelaus (36 B.C.–A.D. 17). Cyprus, originally part of Augustus' province and ruled by an equestrian *pro legato,* had been surrendered to the Senate in 23 B.C., and was now governed by a praetorian proconsul.

Finally there was the great imperial province of Syria, with four legions, ruled by a consular legate. Syria was a curiously discontinuous province, interlaced with kingdoms and tetrarchies. In the hinterland of the Cilician plain was the little Tarcondimotid kingdom, east of it on the Euphrates the kingdom of Commagene. Further south was the kingdom of Emesa, and the surviving parts of Herod's kingdom, under Antipas (4 B.C.–A.D. 39), tetrarch of Galilee and Peraea, and Philip (4 B.C.–A.D. 34) tetrarch of six Ituraean districts. Beyond these was the Nabataean kingdom of Arabia, and the little province of Judaea, governed by an equestrian prefect, who seems to have been independent of the legate of Syria, only calling on him for military aid in a serious emergency.

Augustus thus at the end of his reign had nearly twice as many provinces as the ten other proconsuls, and if some of them, like the two Alpine districts and Judaea, were very small, others like Spain and Syria were very large. The public provinces were on the whole smaller than under the Republic; Baetica was about half the old Hispania Ulterior, Macedonia had included Achaea, and Cyprus had been a minor appendage of Cilicia. The public provinces were on the other hand considerably richer and brought in more revenue, being for the most part civilized areas with highly developed agriculture and some industry. Of Augustus' provinces only Egypt

and Syria were wealthy and productive; the rest were barbarous and recently subdued areas.

The balance was tipped even more strongly in Augustus'
favour by his control of the client kings. Being technically
foreign powers they fell to the share of Augustus, who in
27 B.C. had received the prerogative of declaring war and making treaties. There was only one kingdom in the West, Mauretania, a large but mostly sterile country, but in the East the
kingdoms were numerous. Not all the client rulers were
kings; the title was reserved to the most important only.
Besides the kings there were large numbers of ethnarchs,
tetrarchs and dynasts who ruled petty principalities. Pliny
records that on the provincial register of Syria there were
besides four tetrarchies which he names 'seventeen tetrarchies
with barbarous names distributed into kingdoms' (Pliny,
Natural History V, 82). One of the more important was
Emesa, ruled by the hereditary high priests of Elagabal, a
sacred black meteoric stone. Another priestly principality was
Olba in Cilicia Tracheia, ruled by a priestly dynasty which
claimed descent from the Homeric hero Ajax. Yet another
was Comana in Pontus, a sanctuary of the goddess Enyo. Here
the high priest had been nominated by the kings of Pontus
and now by the Emperor. Directly after Actium, Octavian
appointed a brigand named Cleon who had made himself
useful in Mysia, but he died shortly, struck down by the
goddess for defying her taboo upon pork. Next Augustus put
in a Galatian chieftain, Dyteutus, son of Ateporix.

Of the larger kingdoms some were ruled by native dynasties. In Commagene the royal line went back to the second
century B.C. and claimed descent from the Achaemenids, and
also from Alexander the Great. In Arabia the kings were of
ancient Nabataean descent, the Thracian dynasty was descended from the old royal families of the Astae and the
Sapaei. But the most important kings were creations of
Antonius. Three, Amyntas, Polemo and Archelaus, were
Greek and had no connexion with the kingdoms which were
assigned to them. The fourth, Herod, was not of the Hasmonaean royal line, but was a local man, an Idumean of the
Jewish faith, and son of Antipater, the all powerful vizier of
the last Hasmonaean king.

Royal rule was preferred to provincial administration, according to Strabo, for intractable and unruly areas. A king, being permanent, had a better chance than a Roman governor, who changed every few years, to familiarize himself with the idiosyncrasies of his subjects and learn to manage them. Moreover, being on the spot with his army all the time, he could more promptly check disturbance in the bud than a governor who was often occupied in other parts of his province. This formula did not apply to all client kingdoms; Cappadocia, for instance, was a peaceful area, maintained as a kingdom, it would seem, merely because it always had been one, and perhaps because it had a centralized administrative system unfamiliar to Roman governors. Most however were unruly areas—Mauretania with the Gaetuli; Thrace with the Bessi and other recalcitrant tribes; Galatia, rather prematurely annexed despite the Homonadeis and other restive Pisidian peoples; Cilicia Tracheia, where the Cietae continued to give trouble in Claudius' reign. Herod's kingdom is the classic instance of an intractable area. The religious susceptibilities of the Jews were notoriously acute, and with the best of intentions a Roman governor was liable to provoke a riot; only a native Jew could hope to avoid offence. The Samaritans were always liable to clash with the Jews. The Ituraeans of the northeastern territories normally lived by brigandage.

The kings were generally successful in fulfilling their primary purpose, though occasionally they needed imperial aid, as did Juba on one occasion against the Gaetulians, and the Thracian kings several times against the Bessi. They also did much to introduce a regular administration and even taxation, and establish habits of law and order; Herod's son Philip is highly praised for his paternal rule of his Ituraean subjects. The kings also founded a number of cities to promote the civilization of their kingdoms.

The kings had their own armies, and sometimes fleets also. Herod's army consisted of barbarian mercenaries—regiments of Celts, Germans and Thracians are recorded—and was officered by Romans. With these forces the kings were expected from time to time to assist in imperial wars, as did Rhoemetalces of Thrace in the Pannonian revolt, Polemo and Herod against Bosporus, and Herod and Obodas against Arabia Felix. Some kingdoms had more continuous strategic obligations. Until the annexation of Moesia the Thracian kings were responsible for holding the Haemus frontier, and almost throughout the reign the kings of Pontus, Armenia Minor, Cappadocia and Commagene guarded all the eastern frontier from the Black Sea down to Zeugma in Syria—for Great Armenia even when formally under a client king was very insecure.

It is evident that Augustus had full confidence both in the capacity and the loyalty of his kings. He kept strict discipline among them, deposing those whom he thought unsatisfactory, like Zenodorus of Ituraea and Archelaus of Judaea, and severely reprimanding those who made war on their neighbours without authorization. But he also did his best to foster friendly relations between himself and the kings, and amongst the kings one with another. He encouraged them to send their sons to finish their education at Rome, where they were the guests of prominent senators. He also was a great matchmaker between the sons and daughters of his kings. He thus hoped to build up a happy family of young kings, imbued with loyalty to Rome and linked to one another by ties of marriage and ultimately kinship. On the whole he was successful. Descendants of Herod, Archelaus, Polemo and Rhoemetalces continued to rule various kingdoms for two or three generations, until they were absorbed into the provincial system.

9

The Armed Forces

AUGUSTUS' great achievement in the military field was to create a permanent, standing, professional army, composed both of legions of citizens and of auxiliary cohorts and *alae* of provincials. The army of the Republic had, it is true, moved far in that direction in the last two generations, and this tendency had been accentuated under the dictatorship of Caesar and the triumvirate. Many legions had been kept in being for long periods of years, and the individual men had often served longer, re-enlisting when their original legion was disbanded: centurions in particular often re-enlisted many times up to an advanced age. In principle, however, legions were raised for a given war and disbanded after it, and this was what the men expected.

After Actium Augustus seems to have picked twenty-eight legions out of the fifty-odd at his disposal, disbanding the rest. The twenty-eight became permanent establishments, regularly reinforced as their numbers fell. In exceptional circumstances a legion might be disbanded, if for instance it were completely destroyed by the enemy, like the three—XVII, XVIII and XIX—under Varus, or if it were guilty of gross cowardice or involved in a revolt. Such cases were in fact very rare, and the Augustan legions proved extraordinarily long lived. Of the original twenty-eight sixteen are still listed in the army lists of the *Notitia Dignitatum,* drawn up over four centuries later, and one, V Macedonica, is traceable under Justinian.

Augustus evidently picked his legions from both his own and Antonius' armies, and also must have had at least one of Lepidus' legions amongst his own. The legions are numbered from I to XXII, but four numbers are duplicated—IV Macedonica and IV Scythica, V Alaudae and V Macedonica, VI Ferrata and VI Victrix, and X Gemina and X Fretensis and one—III Augusta, III Cyrenaica and III Gallica—is triplicated; which can only mean that

Augustus had two third legions in his army at Actium, one his own, one taken from Lepidus in 36 B.C., and that he also took over Antonius' third legion. Most of the Augustan legions, apart from the duplicate and triplicate numbers, where they were needed for identification bore nicknames. Some, like Augusta or Victrix, look like official titles, but names like Macedonica were presumably acquired by garrisoning a province for a long period. Gemina denoted a legion formed by the amalgamation of two old legions. Others are clearly pure nicknames but their origin is unknown. The Alaudae (the larks) were a legion recruited from native Gauls by Julius Caesar.

A fixed term of service was laid down from the beginning, at first sixteen years, from A.D. 6 twenty years. This made a solution of the long-standing problem of discharge bounties essential. Ever since Marius had begun recruiting the legions from landless peasants they had demanded allotments of land on which they could live when they were discharged. The Senate had consistently resisted such demands, and it had been left to their commanders to try to satisfy them. The end of every war had thus brought about a major political crisis. The reason for the Senate's opposition is plain enough. The distribution of allotments meant either wholesale confiscation of land, as was done by Sulla and by the triumvirs after Philippi, or a vast expenditure of money to buy land. The discharge bounty of a legionary was fixed at 3000 denarii in A.D. 5. His annual pay at that date was 225 denarii. It therefore cost more than thirteen years' pay to pension a soldier; and it must be remembered that pay covered the whole upkeep of a soldier—rations, clothing, boots and leather equipment, tent, arms, all of which were deducted from his pay.

As he tells us in the *Res Gestae*, for the first thirty years of his reign Augustus bore the enormous cost of veteran settlement out of his own pocket, either paying out cash bounties or buying land in Italy and the provinces; he also, though he does not mention it, used some confiscated provincial land for colonies. This policy was politically advantageous, bringing home to the troops and to the veterans that their welfare depended on Augustus. Eventually however Augustus evidently found it too heavy a burden financially, and handed over the business to the state, establishing a special military treasury. The ordinary revenues were quite inadequate to meet this new recurrent charge, and Augustus insisted, much against the wishes of the Senate, that new taxes must be levied on Roman citizens.

With this improvement in the terms of service, conscription, rare in the late Republic, normally ceased to be necessary. A sensation was caused by the special measures taken after the Pannonian revolt and the Varian disaster, when conscription was applied in Italy. The legions were no doubt, as they were later, largely recruited voluntarily, mainly from sons of veterans.

The praetorian guard and the bulk of the western legions were recruited from Italy, though there was some local enrolment from Africa for the III Augusta, from the Spanish provinces for the Spanish legions, and from Gallia Narbonensis for the German legions. Some of these provincial recruits came from Roman or Latin colonies or municipalities but a fair number from ordinary provincial cities. It is noteworthy that no recruits came from Gallia Comata except from the Roman colony of Lugdunum.

In the East things were very different. The Dalmatian legions drew recruits in large numbers from Macedonia and from all parts of Asia Minor. The Egyptian legions—the only other eastern legions on which we have any substantial information—were almost solidly oriental. In a draft of thirty-six men drawn from III Cyrenaica and XXII Deiotariana there are only three men from the West, and the rest are drawn from Egypt, Cyrenaica, Cyprus, Pamphylia, Pisidia, Paphlagonia, Bithynia and—the largest group of all—Galatia in the narrow sense, the three Gallic tribes. Recruits to the legions were of course supposed to be Roman citizens, but it is evident that both in the West and in the East, but on a larger scale in the East, provincials were recruited and given Roman names and tribes, and deemed to be citizens.

According to some authorities Augustus conferred two useful legal privileges on soldiers, *peculium castrense* and *testamentum militare*. The first meant that a soldier whose father was still living could none the less dispose freely of everything that he acquired in virtue of his military service, that is primarily his pay and his booty; he could even leave it by will. It was a bold inroad into the sacred principle of *patria potestas* thus to give the soldier *filius familias* economic independence. The privilege of the military will was also convenient if less important. It meant that a will made by a soldier was valid despite all technical flaws as long as his intent was plain.

These privileges no doubt encouraged, and were intended to encourage, recruiting. Another rule which Augustus apparently laid down must have had the reverse effect. It seems to have been Augustus who forbade the marriage of soldiers; no soldier might marry, and the existing marriage of a recruit was dissolved. Since the rule was maintained for two centuries, being finally revoked by Septimus Severus, it cannot have caused much discontent, but this was because it was in practice generally ignored. Soldiers married in fact, and the only effect of the rule was to make their children illegitimate —and if they married foreign wives, as they often did, their children would in any case have been illegitimate. Ultimately the prohibition of marriage had the rather odd result of making military service more hereditary, since the bastard sons of soldiers enrolled to obtain the citizenship. But Augustus cannot have foreseen this result—though two soldiers in an Egyptian legion were already born *castris* (i.e. soldiers' bastards) in his reign—and no doubt he was aiming at military efficiency by keeping wives and families out of the camps. He was very chary of allowing even legionary legates, who were of course permitted to marry, to have their wives in camp, and then only in the winter months.

Augustus also made the praetorians a permanent force. Since the middle Republic commanders on campaign had formed a picked *praetoria cohors* as their bodyguard. Augustus kept his in being when he was at Rome, and built it up into a formidable army, nine cohorts, each a thousand strong. According to Suetonius he kept three cohorts only in the city, and billeted the others in neighbouring towns. The praetorians received special privileges. They served at first only twelve years, from A.D. 5 sixteen. Their pay was doubled by the Senate in 27 B.C. and at the time of Augustus' death amounted to 750 denarii, more than three times the legionaries' 225.

The origin of the urban cohorts is obscure. They were numbered in sequence with the praetorians, X, XI and XII, which suggests that they might have been in origin the three praetorian cohorts which Suetonius says Augustus kept in the city, placed under the command of the urban prefect whenever such an officer was appointed. By the end of the reign, however, they were a distinct body, receiving only half the pay of the praetorians.

The only other Roman troops were the cohorts of volunteers and conscripts raised from freeborn and freedmen after the Pannonian revolt and the Varian disaster. These too became permanent establishments. Though organized on military lines in seven cohorts the *vigiles* can hardly be classified as troops: they were recruited from freedmen.

Under the late Republic large numbers of foreign troops had been employed, either sent by client kings and free cities, or levied from the provincial communities. They supplied not only most of the cavalry, in which the Roman army was weak, and specialist arms, such as archers and slingers, but also ordinary infantry. They were naturally recruited from the more warlike areas of the Empire, cavalry from Numidia, Gaul and Spain, slingers from Crete, archers from Syria. They were employed on a purely casual basis, summoned or levied for a campaign and sent home when it was finished. These auxiliary cohorts and *alae* were also converted into permanent establishments by Augustus, and many of them endured for centuries. They were normally commanded by equestrian tribunes and prefects, but sometimes by their native chieftains, like Staius son of Esdragassus, chief of the Trumplini, prefect of the cohort of the Trumplini. We know very little of their conditions of service, but they were certainly much inferior to those of the legions. They served twenty-five years under Claudius, and there is no mention of their receiving any discharge bounty.

Another major achievement of Augustus was the establishment of two standing fleets. The Republic after the middle of the second century B.C. had maintained no fleets and had as a result been plagued with endemic piracy. Augustus created two principal or headquarters fleets (*classes praetoriae*) at Ravenna and Misenum, consisting of triremes for the most part. They were commanded by equestrian prefects, usually former legionary tribunes, but the captains of the ships, following the practice of Sextus Pompeius and the other triumviral commanders of fleets, were Augustus' freedmen or even slaves. The ratings were free provincials recruited mostly from Egypt for the Misenum fleet, from Dalmatia for that of Ravenna. The terms of service were identical with those of the auxiliaries. Augustus probably also created a number of lesser provincial fleets, those of Alexandria in Egypt and of Seleucia in Syria, and three river flotillas, the German on the Rhine, the Pannonian on the middle Danube and the Moesian on the lower Danube. There were also royal fleets, Polemo's in the Black Sea, Herod's at Caesarea; Juba also probably maintained a fleet in the western Mediterranean.

The officer corps was the least satisfactory part of the army, retaining its old amateur character. Augustus brought pressure on all sons of senators and other aspirants to the quaestorship to do some military service. This service was usually the tribunate of a legion, but he is said also to have appointed these young men prefects of *alae*, sometimes sharing the command between two. It seems a very responsible post for a quite inexperienced youth in his early twenties. The great majority of posts at this level, those of tribune of a legion or prefect of a cohort or *ala*, were filled by men of equestrian rank. A few of these were ex-centurions and were of great experience, but the majority were drawn from the upper classes of the Italian cities; Augustus paid much attention to official recommendations from city councils in allocating commissions. Such young men were as inexperienced as aspirants to the Senate, but some of them made themselves into efficient officers by long service. Julius Montanus of Emona served six years as legionary tribune and six as prefect of *alae* before becoming *pro legato* twice. The great majority of equestrian officers, however, seem to have served once or twice only.

The greater experience of such equestrian officers as rose from the centurionate or made a long officer career could not be fully utilized, as all the higher posts were reserved to senators (except in Egypt). Each legion was now commanded by a legate. This was a practice begun by Julius Caesar, who often gave the command of legions or small groups of legions to his legates. Augustus at first sometimes put two legions under one legate, as in Spain, but later established the rule of one legate to one legion. A legionary legate was normally appointed just before or after his praetorship, that is about the age of thirty, having no previous experience except a legionary tribunate about ten years before. If he was to be promoted he would probably serve several years, and after his consulship could be appointed *legatus Augusti pro praetore* of an army of two to four legions. Since senators were excluded from Egypt, the military commands were all held by equestrians here; the prefect of Egypt, with his specially conferred proconsular *imperium*, commanded the whole army, and each of the three legions had an equestrian prefect.

The army seems to have been content on the whole with its conditions of service. There were, it is true, mutinies in Pannonia and Lower Germany immediately after Augustus' death. The men complained of the rate of pay, demanding that it be raised from ten asses a day (225 denarii a year) to one denarius. Another grievance was the many deductions from their pay, for rations, clothing, tents, arms. They showed great animosity against their centurions, accusing them of brutality and of extorting money from their men for granting them leave and excusing them fatigues. They complained that the allotments that they were given on discharge were remote bogs or mountain slopes. But their great grievance was length of service—twenty years officially, but often, they alleged, thirty or forty in practice.

Most of these grievances seem to have had little justification. The rate of pay cannot have been intolerably low, seeing that a hundred years later it remained the same. The pay sheets of two legionaries who served at that time, preserved in an Egyptian papyrus, show that after deductions had been made a soldier could lay by nearly a third of his pay. The excessive length of service was apparently the greatest grievance, for Germanicus thought it wise to reduce the term to sixteen years. Although Tiberius immediately revoked this concession, the mutinies nevertheless fizzled out, and outside Pannonia and Lower Germany there was no trouble.

10

Finance

In the *Res Gestae* Augustus gives a great deal of information about the sums which he spent for public purposes 'from my own money', or 'from my own estate'. On two occasions he specifies that the money came from his share of the war booty (*ex manubiis*), but elsewhere he appears to allude to his purely private resources. The data are incomplete, but in the summary of the *Res Gestae* it is stated that apart from his buildings, and his games, and special benefactions to cities which had suffered from earthquakes and fires, and private gifts to indigent senators and others, he expended 600 million denarii (2,400 million sesterces) on the Roman plebs, discharged soldiers and subventions to the treasury.

When he died he left about 100 million sesterces to the Roman people and the army, besides legacies to friends, and 150 million sesterces to his heirs. This was a fairly substantial fortune, seeing that some senators could not achieve the qualifying fortune of a million or 1,200,000 sesterces, but he apologized for leaving so little to his heirs, and explained that he had spent most of his fortune on the state.

We have no precise information on how Augustus managed to spend such vast sums and still leave so considerable a fortune. He inherited a substantial patrimony from his father and no doubt salvaged a good part of his adoptive father's inheritance. He received large sums in *manubiae*, particularly from Egypt, and he probably accepted crown gold from the provincial cities, though he refused it from those of Italy. But the main source of his wealth was inheritances and legacies. During the last twenty years of his life he received 1,400 million sesterces in this way.

The subventions which Augustus made to the state were undoubtedly a useful supplement to the public revenues, but they were a very small percentage of them. The figures are unfortunately very dubious, but it would appear that Pompeius at his triumph in 61 B.C. claimed that he had by his conquests (of Bithynia, Pontus, Cilicia and Syria) increased the provincial revenue from 50 to 85 million denarii; Caesar is said to have brought in 40 million sesterces from Gaul, and Augustus the same from Egypt; it seems very little, but doubtless excluded the considerable revenue in corn. Augustus' later conquests—the Alpine provinces, Raetia, Noricum, Pannonia and Moesia—were all poor districts which cannot have yielded much, but his general reorganization of provincial taxation doubtless increased its yield. The revenues from the provinces in the latter part of his reign may well have amounted to 250 million denarii a year, beside which his private contribution (excluding luxuries like buildings and games) averaged barely 15 millions.

It is generally accepted on rather meagre evidence that Augustus transformed provincial taxation and introduced the system which prevailed under the later principate. Under the late Republic provinces fell into two classes, those which like Spain and Gaul paid *stipendium,* and those like Sicily and Asia which paid tithe and pasture dues. *Stipendium* was a fixed money contribution, imposed on each community. It was apparently more or less arbitrarily assessed, for no provincial census is ever mentioned under the Republic, and must often have been very inequitable, some cities being under-assessed and others too heavily burdened. The *stipendia* were probably directly collected by the governor or his quaestor from the city governments. The tithe was ideally fairer, since it ought to have varied according to the actual crop harvested each year by each landowner, but it was necessarily, since the yield varied from year to year and was unpredictable, farmed to contractors (*publicani*), who took advantage of their political influence to extract vastly greater sums than were really due. For the *publicani* were leading members of the equestrian order, which the Senate normally wished to placate and which moreover dominated the court of provincial extortion, before which any governor who resisted them could be brought to trial. There was one province which fell in neither class, Africa, where the provincials paid a fixed land tax and a poll tax. The land tax was possible because all Africa had been surveyed and the area of every farm was thus known. The poll tax was apparently collected by contractors, because no count of the population was kept.

Julius Caesar had started a reform in Asia, where he abolished the tithe and the contracting companies, and made the cities collect a fixed tax based on the average yield of the tithe less a third. The rebate was probably intended to compensate for the fact that the companies habitually overbid grossly to obtain the contract, knowing that they could easily recoup themselves by exaggerating their estimate of the crop. Caesar's system was more equitable than the old, but remained very rough and ready.

In the system which prevailed in the later principate and which Augustus probably introduced, *stipendium* and tithe had disappeared and there were two main taxes, *tributum capitis*, which was a poll tax, paid in some provinces by all adults, and in others only by adult males, and *tributum soli*, a land tax, which probably also took in other capital assets, such as houses and ships—these certainly paid tax under one heading or the other. These taxes were based on regularly recurrent censuses, in which the population was counted and the land—and other property—registered in detail. The tax payable by each taxpayer—a fixed sum per head for *tributum capitis* and a percentage of the assessed value of the property for *tributum soli*—was thus equitably determined, and as the amount was known in advance it was collected not by contractors but by the city authorities. By accurately assessing the taxable wealth of the provinces Augustus was able to extract more revenue—as he is recorded to have done in Asia and Bithynia-Pontus—without causing hardship. The principal reason for believing that Augustus did introduce this system is that he is recorded, for the first time in history, to have conducted provincial censuses, in Gaul in 27 B.C. and 13 B.C., in Syria, through his legate Quirinius, in A.D. 6.

Besides the direct taxation on the provinces there were as under the Republic the customs dues, levied at the frontiers of the Empire at twenty-five per cent and at provincial boundaries at two per cent or two-and-a-half per cent. These were still collected by contractors since their yield was unpredictable. The new tax imposed by **Augustus on Roman citizens,** the five per cent duty on inheritances, earmarked for the military treasury, was farmed to contractors for the same reason as the customs.

The financial organization of the Empire under Augustus is even more obscure than the taxation system. Under the later Republic the Senate had been in control of finance and the urban quaestors could make no payment from the treasury (*aerarium*) except by decree of the Senate. In theory all revenues were paid into the *aerarium* by the tax contractors and the governors of provinces which paid *stipendia,* and the Senate voted annual allowances from the *aerarium* to provincial governors for the payment of their assistants and of the troops and for purchases of supplies. In actual practice, to avoid unnecessary transport of coin, an outgoing governor normally received not cash but a draft on the tax contractors of his province, and returned any balance to them: the tax contractors presumably had their obligations to the treasury correspondingly adjusted. It may be conjectured that in provinces which paid *stipendia,* these were normally held in the provincial treasury (*fiscus*) and that governors drew their allowances from their *fisci,* only remitting surpluses to Rome. Each governor had of course to account with the *aerarium* for the sums which he received and spent and refunded. The *aerarium* was thus mainly a clearing house, though it was also a storehouse for accumulated balances of coin, and could if necessary make issues of coin. The extraordinary provincial commands of the late Republic were apparently similarly financed with annual grants, but under the *lex Gabinia* Pompeius was authorized to draw the grant from any company of tax contractors or provincial *fiscus* that he found convenient. This was presumably because his operations against the pirates covered almost the whole of the Empire.

There is no evidence on the point at all, but it is a natural assumption that Augustus followed the precedents of the later Republic. In that case the Senate, when it assigned and periodically renewed his group of provinces, would have voted him an appropriate annual grant, and since his provinces were widely dispersed it may have extended to him the provisions of the *lex Gabinia,* allowing him to draw from any tax contracting company or provincial *fiscus.* Augustus would naturally have found it most convenient to draw first from the *fisci* of his own provinces, but as his provinces were, with the exception of Egypt, rather poor, and his expenses, including most of the army, very heavy, he must have drawn part of his grant from other sources. Some, no doubt, such as the maintenance of the praetorian and urban cohorts, and in the last few years of his reign the expenses of the Roman corn supply, he must have drawn direct from the *aerarium*. He may also have drawn from the *fisci* of public provinces, and from the contractors of the provincial customs.

How far Augustus accounted for his grant is obscure. He need not have done so constitutionally, since he never retired from his provincial command, but he may well have thought it politic to do so. This is suggested by the statement that Gaius 'published the accounts of the Empire which Augustus had been used to post up, but Tiberius had omitted to do so' (Suetonius, *Caligula* 16, 1). We are told of only two occasions when Augustus did present accounts, and these were very special occasions, in 23 B.C. when he thought he was going to die and handed them to his fellow consul, and at his death in A.D. 14. But on the second occasion the accounts are said to have been of the whole Empire, and included statements of the money in the *aerarium* and the provincial *fisci* and in the hands of the tax contractors, and also the strength of all the troops. These documents do not look like official magistrate's accounts, but unofficial statistical surveys which he maintained as head of the Empire. It may be then that he periodically published his own official accounts, and kept a confidential statistical survey of the whole Empire.

As far as management went Augustus drew no distinction between his private fortune and his public funds, though he clearly distinguished them carefully in his accounting. He appointed an agent or bailiff (*procurator*) in each province, whether public or his own. In the public provinces they were concerned only with the management of his private estates, in his own provinces they also collected the revenue and paid the troops. They were sometimes his freedmen—a famous case is Licinus in Gaul—but more often men of equestrian rank, usually ex-officers. They were presumably assisted by staffs of clerks and accountants, freedmen and slaves of Augustus, like Musicus, slave of Tiberius, who is recorded in the next reign as 'cashier of the Gallic *fiscus* of the province of Lugdunensis' (Ehrenberg and Jones, *Documents* 158).

At Rome Augustus must have had a central accounting staff, and since the three public clerks (*scribae*) to which he and his two quaestors were entitled would have been quite inadequate for the vast volume of work involved, even if efficient, he no doubt employed his own freedmen and slaves, as did Tiberius after him, under whom is recorded Antemus, freedman of Tiberius Caesar Augustus, chief accountant (*a rationibus*).

Augustus' system of taxation, though a great improvement on what had gone before, was not perfect. The *tributum soli*, being assessed on capital, did not touch those who lived by salaries or fees, like doctors, rhetoricans and grammarians, and lawyers; and some of them were very rich. It also let off too lightly merchants, whose capital assets, such as ships, did not represent their true wealth. For the great majority of taxpayers, who were landowners, and especially the humblest among them, the peasant proprietors, it could be oppressive. It was a fixed sum, which had to be paid every year, whether the harvest was good, average or bad, and in Mediterranean lands harvests are very variable. It was not progressive, and a humble peasant paid at the same rate as a wealthy landowner. The *tributum capitis*, which was paid by the poorest—and from which privileged categories like Alexandrians in Egypt were immune—was a highly inequitable tax. It might mean that a poor peasant with a large family paid more than a neighbour who had a larger holding but was a bachelor.

The general effect of all these faults in the system was that the rich, the great landowners, were undertaxed, because a higher rate would have been utterly ruinous for the peasantry, and that the peasantry nevertheless were hard-pressed in bad years. In Augustus' time the rate seems to have been low, so that the rich were very prosperous and the peasants tolerably comfortable. After Vespasian had raised rates all round, and in some cases doubled them, there are signs of serious distress among the peasantry.

In the face of strong opposition Augustus did something to reduce the inequitable fiscal privileges of Roman citizens.

FINANCE

It would appear that Romans throughout the Empire were exempt from *tributum capitis*. Those who owned land in Italy, and in some at any rate of the transmarine colonies, were also exempt from *tributum soli*. About a dozen of Augustus' colonies in the provinces are recorded to have possessed this privilege, the *ius Italicum*, but our list is far from exhaustive, and it would seem that he was generous to his veterans.

It would have been the fairest course to impose *tributum capitis* and *tributum soli* on all citizens, but this would have been politically impossible. Augustus' solution was to impose new taxes, notably the five per cent tax on inheritances, on all citizens. This was unfair on citizens who owned land in the provinces, and in particular on provincials who received the citizenship, who had now to pay the inheritance tax on top of the normal provincial land tax, and were excused only the poll tax, which was a negligible item for the well-to-do provincials who normally received the citizenship.

Justice

UNDER the late Republic, crimes committed in Italy were tried in public courts (*iudicia publica* or *quaestiones*) at Rome, presided over by praetors or ex-aediles, styled *iudex quaestionis*; the verdict was given by juries of *iudices*. Augustus added a new court for adultery, but did not otherwise make any important change in the system. Since 70 B.C. the jurors had been drawn equally from three panels (*decuriae*), consisting of senators, *equites* (freeborn citizens possessing 400,000 sesterces or over) and *tribuni aerarii,* apparently a class of lower property qualification. Julius Caesar had abolished the panel of *tribuni aerarii.* Under Augustus there were three decuries of *equites*; senators certainly still served, but apparently in the three decuries of *equites,* where they would have formed a very small minority, since under Augustus each decury was close on one thousand strong. Augustus took great pains with the recruitment of the panels. He sometimes selected the members himself, probably in virtue of the censorial powers he held from time to time: we also hear of the consul of 12 B.C. being armed with censorial power for the purpose. He found some difficulty in getting men to serve. He had to lower the qualifying age from thirty-five to thirty. He had also to create a judicial vacation in November and December. And finally he had to allow one of the three decuries to be freed from judicial duties each year in rotation.

These courts continued to function, though some of the more important cases which should have gone to them came to be deflected to the new courts mentioned below. Augustus had no direct control over them except the 'vote of Minerva', granted to him in 30 B.C., which enabled him to pardon those whom they had condemned. The *quaestiones* covered certain crimes only, most of them political, treason, speculation, extortion, electoral corruption, riot, some private, murder, forgery and adultery. Other crimes were left to the magistrates to punish, and against their sentences, except for small fines, there was in theory an appeal to the people (*provocatio ad populum*), leading to a trial before the assembly. Some time before A.D. 58, when Paul appealed to Caesar, *provocatio ad populum* had become *appellatio ad Caesarem*. It is probable that the change happened under Augustus. It may be that the tribunician power to give *auxilium* to all who called upon him and to judge an appeal, which is coupled by Dio with the vote of Minerva amongst the powers which were voted to Octavian in 30 B.C., denotes the transfer of *provocatio* from the people to the emperor.

Augustus added two new criminal courts to the *iudicia publica*, the consuls sitting with the Senate, and himself, naturally sitting with his *consilium*. The senatorial court was certainly well established by A.D. 8, when Ovid alludes to it as a normal alternative to the *quaestiones*. It does not seem to have existed as early as 23 B.C., when the cases of Primus, Murena and Caepio, which would by later usage have come before it, were tried by the *iudicia publica*. The evidence for the imperial court is much less firm, consisting mostly of anecdotes, but Tiberius accepted it as an established institution in A.D. 17, and he was always careful to observe Augustan precedent.

These two courts were courts of voluntary jurisdiction. It was for the accuser to request the consuls or the emperor to take the case, and they might refuse. To judge by later practice the senatorial court was normally used for political crimes, and for ordinary crimes of senators and women of senatorial rank. The imperial court seems to have had a wider scope. We hear of Augustus trying a case of parricide, and endeavouring by leading questions to prevent the accused from confessing, which would make him liable to the antique and gruesome penalty of being sewn into a sack with a dog, a cock, a viper and a monkey, and then hurled into the sea. We also hear of him trying a case of a forged will, and exempting the innocent witnesses from the penalties of the law. On another occasion an accuser asks him to receive a charge of murder against a quaestor, on the ground that the accused's counsel, Germanicus, would exercise undue influence on the jurors of the *quaestio de sicariis*. This is the only recorded case where a senator was accused, and Augustus refused it. He is recorded to have taken only one political case, and here the accused was a person of no importance, one Aemilius Aelianus of Corduba, and the political charge—slander against Augustus—was one of several, and evidently dragged in merely to create prejudice.

The new consular court was, like some others of Augustus' innovations, an antiquarian revival. As holders of the highest *imperium* the consuls were supremely qualified to exercise capital justice, but they had very rarely done so, and then only in virtue of a *senatus consultum* to deal with a crisis. The consuls had so acted in 132 and 121 B.C. to punish the adherents of Tiberius and Gaius Gracchus, and their action had been strongly condemned by the *populares* as a violation of the citizens' right of appeal (*provocatio ad populum*). This right had been reaffirmed by the *lex Sempronia* of 123 B.C. Since then Cicero had executed the Catilinarian conspirators, but he had been exiled for his action—and later recalled. The right of *provocatio* had finally been secured by Caesar in his *lex Iulia de vi publica*. Augustus could hardly have ignored this last enactment, and it must be presumed that he obtained legislative sanction for his new consular court, excepting it from appeal, perhaps by his *lex Iulia de iudiciis publicis privatisque*. Augustus' main object no doubt in establishing the consular court was to keep political crimes and the trials of important persons—such cases as those of Cornelius Gallus, Primus, Murena and Caepio—within his control. For though the consuls presided and the Senate formed the jury, Augustus could attend and exercise his authority, for voting was normally open.

Augustus' own court was probably based on the consular *imperium* which he enjoyed from 19 B.C. and was thus strictly parallel with the court of the consuls and the Senate. It is less easy to see what purpose it served, and it seems in fact to have been of little importance in this period.

Augustus established another minor criminal court at Rome, that of the prefect of the city. It was primarily concerned with petty crime and dealt largely with foreigners and slaves, but did also punish humble citizens. It must therefore, like the two higher criminal courts, have been exempted from *provocatio*. The prefect's court must have fulfilled a long felt want in providing speedy repression of crime, which was rife in the heterogeneous and crowded population of Rome. Its range of activity gradually increased until by Nero's reign it had apparently taken over much of the business of the *iudicia publica*.

For practical purposes in the Republic the death penalty had ceased to exist for citizens. Those convicted on a capital charge were 'forbidden fire and water' and went into exile in a foreign city of their own choice, retaining their property. In A.D. 12 Augustus made the penalty a little severer. Exiles were not allowed to go to a mainland city, nor to an island within fifty miles of the coast, except for Cos, Lesbos, Rhodes and Sardinia. On their island they were not allowed to own more than one merchant ship, or have more than twenty slaves or freedmen, nor to own more than 500,000 sesterces. These rules, which left a condemned criminal more than the minimum qualification for the equestrian order, do not seem very harsh.

In the provinces criminal jurisdiction had under the Republic been exercised over provincials by the governor, sitting with his *consilium*; he could not execute a capital sentence on a Roman citizen, but presumably had to remit him to Rome, unless he rode roughshod over the law. In 6 B.C. we find criminal jury courts, like the *iudicia publica*, existing in Cyrenaica, the juries consisting of resident Romans of a modest property qualification; they apparently tried not only provincials but Romans. This is the only record that we have of such courts, and we do not know whether they existed in other provinces, nor when they were established and when they ceased to function. It is plausible to suggest that they were created both to provide better criminal justice for the provincials than the no doubt often arbitrary judgment of the governor, subject only to the advice of assessors whom he chose himself, and also to make it possible for the governor to deal with the crimes of resident Romans; for such a court could be reasonably exempted from appeal to the people. These courts probably dealt only with the crimes which came under the public courts at Rome (*crimina iudiciorum publicorum*), for there were cases which the governor of Cyrenaica still tried himself in the old way: in these cases there would be an appeal to Caesar. If this reconstruction is correct, Roman citizens in the provinces lost their virtual immunity from criminal proceedings, and provincials got a fairer form of trial—unless, as actually happened in Cyrene, the Roman residents conspired to convict them on false charges.

In civil justice under the Republic all cases in Italy, except those of minor importance which were tried by the city magistrates, went first to the urban praetor (or if a foreigner was involved to the peregrine praetor) at Rome, who after discussion with the litigants or their counsel laid down a *formula*, defining the legal issues, and appointed a private citizen (*iudex privatus*) or citizens (*recuperatores*) to judge the issue of fact and pronounce sentence. In the provinces the governor could take a case himself, but normally the same procedure was followed as in Italy, the case going in the first instance to the provincial governor or one of his legates, who pronounced a *formula* and appointed a judge or judges. In some provinces, such as Sicily, there were rules governing the choice of judges, whether they should be Romans or provincials, and if the latter, from the same or other cities. In other provinces, as in Asia, Cilicia and Cyrenaica, the governor apparently had an unrestricted choice. It is not clear what the rule about judges was in Italy, but unless the two parties agreed on a man of their choice, members of decuries were apparently usually selected.

There was under the Republic only a very rudimentary form of appeal. A litigant who thought the *formula* unfair or the *iudex* prejudiced could appeal from the praetor to a tribune of the plebs, or to an equal or greater power, i.e. another praetor or a consul. A tribune, having no power of jurisdiction, could in response only veto the case until the praetor altered his *formula* or chose another *iudex*. A consul, and probably also a praetor, could not only veto the proceedings, but try the case himself. In the provinces, where there were no tribunes and the governor had no colleagues, it was only possible for an aggrieved litigant to ask for *revocatio Romae,* and there was nothing to make the governor send his case to Rome. Both in Italy and in the provinces, it would seem, appeals lay only from the magistrate—the praetor or the governor—and no appeal was possible from the judge: at any rate none are recorded in our sources.

Augustus himself exercised civil jurisdiction in the first instance, presumably in virtue of his consular *imperium*. Those who brought their cases to him were, it seems, persons who had no remedy under the praetor's edict. We hear of a man who had been disinherited at birth by his father, though he had no complaint either against him or his mother. In another case two brothers had been cut out of the will of their widowed mother, who had married an elderly man. This was clearly against the spirit of the *lex Iulia de maritandis ordinibus*, and Augustus gave them the estate and made the elderly second husband refund them their mother's dowry.

It does not appear that these rather arbitrary judgments created precedents, but in another matter, that of *fideicommissa*, Augustus not only legalized a practice which had become common, though it had not received the protection of the praetor's edict, but introduced a new jurisdiction, or rather revived the long dormant jurisdiction of the consuls, to enforce the new rule. People had adopted the practice of inserting in their wills *fideicommissa*, that is requests to their heirs to make various dispositions, to pay sums of money to individuals or convey property to them or to free slaves: this was often done to evade legal obstacles of a technical character. Such clauses were considered morally binding, but the praetor refused to enforce them, and some heirs ignored them. Augustus used his consular authority in a number of cases to enforce *fideicommissa*, and eventually requested the consuls to take on the jurisdiction.

In the appointment of judges Augustus may have made a change. The *decuriae* of judges are sometimes described as *publicis privatisque*, which implies that their members were officially enrolled to be not only jurors in the criminal courts, but judges in private suits. Furthermore, in A.D. 4 he created a fourth decury, with a smaller property qualification (200,000 sesterces), to try minor cases. These clearly were judges in private suits, and their creation implies that the selection of judges was confined to the decuries.

By far the most important change which Augustus introduced into the judicial system was the vast extension of appeal. Appeals now ran not only from the magistrates but from *iudices privati,* both from Italy and from the provinces. They could go to the Senate, or more strictly the consuls, who had a *maius imperium* over the praetors and provincial governors, but the vast majority went to Augustus, presumably in virtue of his *maius imperium* over other proconsuls, his superior *imperium* over his own *legati pro praetore,* and the consular *imperium* in Italy which he acquired in 19 B.C. The volume of appeals became so great that he had to delegate them, those from Italy to the urban praetor, those from the provinces to a consular appointed for each.

The facility of appeal must have remedied many injustices and reversed many erroneous decisions. The fact that the bulk of appeals went to Augustus must also have settled many dubious points of law and eliminated many anomalies and contradictions. For Augustus presumably followed his own precedents, and magistrates and judges naturally followed them also, knowing that any contrary judgment would be upset on appeal.

A strong force was thus set in motion making for the certainty and uniformity of the law. In another way also Augustus contributed to this end. One of the sources of the law under the Republic had been the *responsa prudentium,* the answers given to legal problems by those who were regarded as experts in the law. These, of course, might well conflict, and there was no means of telling which expert was in the right. Augustus did not interfere with this practice, but he did give his official approval to certain *prudentes* and his *auctoritas* was thereby conferred upon them.

Social Policy

IT can be seen from the contemporary poets, especially Horace and Ovid, that among the upper classes at Rome standards of sexual morality were very lax. The marriage tie was lightly regarded, and adultery was tolerated and indeed fashionable. Marriage itself was unpopular, and many men and women preferred to remain unmarried. Children were regarded as a nuisance, and many marriages were childless. These habits encouraged the activities of fortune hunters, who became almost a regular profession, and by their attentions made the life of the unmarried or childless an attractive one. Wild extravagance was also rife, and enormous sums were spent on exotic luxuries. It may be doubted whether these vices extended to the lower classes at Rome, still less to the Italian towns, but their prevalence in high Roman society no doubt created the impression that the Roman people as a whole was in dire need of reform.

Augustus tackled these problems in 18 B.C., using his tribunician power to introduce the necessary legislation. To the problem of extravagance Augustus made the usual response of a sumptuary law, limiting expenditure on meals, clothes, plate, jewellery and the like. Like all sumptuary laws it soon became a dead letter. For the protection of marriage he passed the *lex Iulia de adulteriis coercendis*. Adultery had always been a crime in Roman law, tried by a magistrate, usually an aedile, before the assembly, but it had never been furnished with a *iudicium publicum*, and prosecutions had lapsed in the last years of the Republic. Augustus revised the law, probably making it milder. No proceedings could be taken unless the husband first divorced his suspected wife, and then he, or the wife's father, had the exclusive right of prosecution for sixty days, after which any accuser could bring the charge. The penalties were severe on both guilty parties, relegation to different islands with loss of half or a third of their property. *Stuprum*, that is intercourse between a man and any woman not his wife or a registered prostitute, was also brought under the scope of the law. Most important of all a regular *quaestio* was set up.

To encourage marriage and the procreation of children Augustus passed the *lex Iulia de maritandis ordinibus*. As this law was extensively modified by the *lex Papia Poppaea* of A.D. 9 its provisions are not easy to distinguish. It made illegal various restrictions on marriage, but prohibited the marriage of senators or their descendants down to great grandsons and great granddaughters with freedwomen or actresses or their daughters. It penalized the unmarried or childless of both sexes by making them incapable of taking inheritances or legacies except from close relations, and it benefited men and women with children by various privileges, including seniority under the *leges annales* for holding magistracies. The highest privileges went to women with three, or if freedwomen four, children. Augustus also tried to curb frivolous divorces by enacting that a divorce was not valid unless witnessed by seven persons. The clauses of the *lex Iulia de maritandis ordinibus* voiding legacies and bequests caused immense resentment among the Roman upper classes. Legacies and bequests to friends were very common, and the unmarried and childless deeply resented being deprived of them. They seem also to have urged that it was inequitable to penalize married persons who were unfortunate enough to have no children. At length in A.D. 9 the agitation came to a head. The *equites* made a demonstration in the theatre, and Augustus summoned them to the Forum, where he made the bachelors stand on one side, and the married and those with children on the other, and harangued each group in turn. He was obliged, however, to make some concessions, and a law, the *lex Papia Poppaea*, was introduced by the two consuls, who were unfortunately both bachelors. This apparently reduced or removed the disabilities of the married but childless, and increased the rewards of parents with children. According to Tacitus it had little effect in raising the birthrate, but merely enriched the treasury with a flow of *caduca*, that is estates left to persons disqualified by the law from taking them and therefore lapsing to the state. It also gave much employment to informers, who detected breaches of the law and received rewards for successful prosecutions.

Another social problem was the excessive and indiscriminate manumission of slaves, or rather the massive influx of freed slaves into the citizen body. The legislation did not affect slaves freed informally (*inter amicos* or *per epistolam*), who remained legally slaves though their liberty was protected by the praetor, but only those manumitted *vindicta* or *censu* or by will, who became Roman citizens. The legislation was not in this case proposed by Augustus himself, but by the consuls, Fufius Geminus and Caninius Gallus in 2 B.C. and Aelius Catus and Sentius Saturninus in A.D. 4. The *lex Fufia Caninia* limited testamentary manumission, which was liable to be very indiscriminate, since the testator could thereby display his generosity and benevolence at no cost to himself. An owner of two slaves could free both, an owner of three to ten half the number, and so on until a man who owned 100 to 500 could free only one fifth, and no one over 100. The slaves had to be individually named in the will and any manumissions in excess of the legal maximum were void.

The *lex Aelia Sentia* dealt with the manumissions *inter vivos*. No owner under twenty might manumit unless he could show good cause before a *consilium* of five senators and five *equites* at Rome, or twenty Roman citizens in the provinces; manumissions made contrary to this rule were void, and so were those made by the will of an owner under twenty. No slave might be legally freed, except with the approval of a *consilium*, if he or she was under thirty; but in this case the slave was informally freed, though denied the citizenship. Another clause declared that slaves who had been branded or tortured or trained as gladiators, and presumably therefore had a criminal record, should if manumitted be relegated to a new class of freedmen, *peregrini dediticii*, whose main disability was that they were for ever debarred from the Roman citizenship.

According to Suetonius (*Augustus* 40, 3) Augustus 'thought it important to keep the people pure and uncontaminated by all corruption of foreign and servile blood'. The situation must indeed have seemed alarming, for owing to the constant wars slaves came on the market in vast numbers—the bulk of the Astures and the Cantabri, for instance, were enslaved, and all the Salassi—and manumissions increased correspondingly. There is, however, evidence that Augustus was not a racialist. He positively encouraged freedmen and freedwomen to breed. A freedwoman who bore four children gained valuable legal privileges, and a slave manumitted under thirty could acquire Roman citizenship simply by marrying a freeborn Roman woman or a freedwoman of Roman status or of his own, and in due course registering a one-year-old child; the citizenship was also accorded to his wife, if not a Roman already, and to the child. Augustus evidently believed that freed slaves of foreign extraction could in time make good citizens, and that their children certainly could. He only wanted to reduce the influx of freed slaves into the citizen body to a more gradual flow.

Suetonius also says that for similar reasons Augustus was chary of giving citizenship to provincials. As evidence he only cites two anecdotes, that he told Tiberius that he must personally make a good case for a Greek whom he had recommended, and that he refused the citizenship to a Gaul recommended by Livia, and gave him immunity from taxation, saying he preferred to incur a financial loss rather than vulgarize the honour of the Roman citizenship. It is difficult to check Suetonius' statement. Some of the large number of Gaii Julii found throughout the provinces must be due to Augustus, though more perhaps owed their name to his adoptive father. It is also difficult to check how liberal Augustus was in converting provincial cities into *oppida civium Romanorum* or giving them Latin status, whereby their annual magistrates obtained the citizenship. Julius Caesar had done both on a lavish scale, and it is difficult and in many cases impossible to distinguish his work from that of Augustus. His treatment of the Sicilians in 36 B.C., when he abolished their municipal status wholesale except for Rome's oldest ally Messina, suggests that he disapproved of his father's policy; but in the same year he made Utica an *oppidum civium Romanorum*, presumably for timely desertion of Lepidus. Suetonius also states that he gave citizenship or Latin rights to a number of the cities which claimed to have done service to the Roman people. It is however significant that among the written precepts he left to his successor was 'to check manumissions to prevent filling the city with an alien mob, and not to admit many persons to the citizenship, to maintain the distinction between themselves and their subjects' (Cassius Dio LVI, 33).

It would be interesting, if it were possible, to check these vague conclusions by the population figures given by Augustus' three censuses. They are 4,063,000 in 28 B.C., 4,233,000 in 8 B.C. and 4,937,000 in A.D. 14. They thus show a decennial increment of two per cent in the first twenty years of Augustus' principate, and of eight per cent in the last twenty-one years. These figures, of course, could and probably do, represent a gradual annual rise in increment, but steeper in the second half of the reign.

One must first ask what the figures represent. A Roman census had under the Republic, in theory at any rate, made a count of all adult male citizens, over eighteen years of age, wherever resident: there was also a supplementary list of orphan boys and girls and widows who owned property. The last Republican census in 70 B.C. had produced a figure of 910,000, and as it is impossible that the population can have more than quadrupled itself in the next forty years, it is believed by some scholars that Augustus altered the basis of the census, including women. It is true that some women's names are quoted from the imperial census lists, but these could well be from the supplementary schedule and it seems very unlikely that Augustus, reviving a moribund Republican institution as a prelude to the restoration of the old Republic, would have made so gratuitous an innovation. There are various explanations of the enormous apparent increase. In the first place the Republican census had been very inefficient. Citizens, even though they lived at Tarentum or Aquileia or overseas, were expected to declare themselves either in person or through a legal representative in Rome, and many poor citizens in the remoter parts of Italy no doubt failed to register. Now, under a law of Caesar, the declarations were made in the municipalities. There was therefore a much more thorough count of citizens. New citizens were moreover created not only by natural increase but by manumission of slaves and the grant of citizenship to foreigners.

Manumission was lavish at this period, as Augustus' later legislation shows, and Caesar and the triumvirs had been very generous in granting citizenship not only to individuals but to whole provincial communities. This would have added very substantially to the total.

On the whole the natural increase was slow in the ancient world, owing to the very high death rate, not only in infancy and childhood, but in adult years. Two per cent is probably a fairly good rate of increase, and hardly implies that the birthrate was as low as Augustus thought it was. At the same time it suggests that grants of citizenship must have been sparing and that manumission could have been very excessive. The much higher rate in the latter part of the reign is unlikely to indicate more liberal grants of citizenship, for Augustus seems to have become more sparing as he grew older. It might reflect the effects of the *lex Iulia de maritandis ordinibus*—an increased birthrate from 18 B.C. onwards would begin to affect the census figures in A.D. 1. It might also reflect increased manumissions, the result of increased wealth and larger slave households; the phenomenon first attracted Augustus' notice in 2 B.C. Peace and the increased prosperity of Italy and the colonies and *municipia* in the provinces may also have led to a greater natural increase, not so much by a higher birth rate as by a higher survival rate among children. This would not appear in the census lists until about 10 B.C.

Augustus, it would seem, like most upper-class Romans, believed in a society stratified by birth and wealth, but with a limited degree of social mobility. At the top came the senators, whose function it was to guide the state by their counsels, govern the provinces and command the army. Here Augustus for the first time laid down a qualification of property, and gave the first official sanction to the hereditary principle by allowing sons of the senators to wear the broad stripe and attend sessions of the house. Senatorial blood was kept untainted by the ban on marriage with freedwomen and the like. On the other hand he seems to have encouraged 'all the flower of the municipalities and colonies' of Italy to enter the Senate, no doubt easing their advancement by *commendatio*.

The second order of the state, the *ordo equester*, was a

more amorphous body, and its public function less clearly defined. The word *eques* was used ambiguously in two different senses. Strictly speaking the equestrian order comprised only the eighteen centuries of *equites equo publico*, which had long ago ceased to have any military function and were merely voting units in the *comitia centuriata*. Qualifications were free birth, property of 400,000 sesterces or over, and relative youth—under forty-five. Augustus enlarged the group from 1800 to about 5000, and seems to have tried to give it a more military flavour. He organized the eighteen centuries into six squadrons (*turmae*), which were led by six officers (*seviri*), usually young nobles before they entered the Senate. He also revived the annual march past (*travectio*), in which *equites* led their horses past the consuls and were inspected. Augustus held these parades himself, presumably in virtue of his consular power. He also held periodical revisions of the roll of the *equites*, assisted by a committee of ten senators, and endeavoured to raise their moral tone by punishing or marking with ignominy those guilty of unseemly conduct. The mildest form of rebuke was to hand a note in the presence of the committee to the victim, which he had to read himself in their presence. Augustus also tried to reduce the average age of *equites*. In 13 B.C. he compulsorily enrolled qualified men under thirty-five who were physically fit, and he encouraged those over thirty-five who were infirm to resign. This insistence on physical fitness again emphasized the military character of the *equites equo publico*.

All freeborn persons possessed of 400,000 sesterces seem also to have been called *equites*, not only in popular language, but sometimes officially, and to have enjoyed certain equestrian privileges, such as the gold ring and the first fourteen rows at the theatre. Pliny says that Augustus confined the title *eques* and the gold ring to the *equites equo publico*, but this must have been a short-lived reform. From this larger body were drawn the judges of the three decuries; not many *equites equo publico* can have served on them, as the age limit was over thirty-five, later over thirty. The posts of military tribune or prefect were also called *equestres militiae*, but whether the public horse or the property qualification was required is not known.

Augustus employed a number of *equites* in higher military posts of his own creation, and also in civilian capacities. On the military side there were the prefects of the fleets, of the Egyptian legions, of the *vigiles* and of the praetorians; the last two posts were of higher rank, and the praetorian prefects very important. On the civil side there were half a dozen judicial and financial posts in Egypt, the prefectures of small provinces like the Alpine districts or Judaea, and at a higher level the prefecture of the *annona* at Rome, and the prefecture of Egypt, the most important equestrian post in the Empire. These were all government appointments. Besides these, there were Augustus' private financial agents, the procurators.

The number of posts was very small—about forty in all—and no regular pattern of promotion is traceable. An ambitious young *eques* first held a commission or two in the army as tribune or prefect, and having earned testimonials from his provincial governor might apply for one of the middle grade posts. So Aulus Castrienus after serving as military tribune and *praefectus alae* became prefect of the fleet, and Lucius Volusenus after three military commissions was sent to Egypt as *iuridicus*. Quintus Octavius made a longer career. After two commissions he served four years as procurator in Raetia (when that province was still under a legate), ten years in Spain and two years in Syria, where he died. There is no evidence that procurators and the like were promoted to higher posts like the Roman prefectures and that of Egypt, which were often filled by personal friends of Augustus.

The equestrian order is generally envisaged as a class of businessmen and financiers. It is true that under the Republic the contractors for the revenues were drawn from the *equites*, and that *equites* did a vast moneylending business in the provinces—though here they had competition from senators. But these businessmen must have been a minority in the order, which consisted mostly of landowners in the Italian towns, men like Cicero of Arpinum. The abolition of the farming system for the provincial tithes must have deprived a limited number of *equites* of very considerable profits, and with peace and better government the provincial cities had less need of loans—though debt was the principal cause of the rebellion of Gaul in A.D. 21. But the average member of the equestrian order would have been little affected. Apart from the very limited numbers who became procurators of Augustus or held military or administrative prefectures, the *equites* were a class of landed gentry, some of whom held two or three military commissions in their youth, and in their later years served as jurors.

Below the Senate and the equestrian order came the plebs. Even within the plebs there was a hierarchy, which Augustus emphasized, between the freeborn and freedmen. Freedmen had always been excluded from public office and the Senate, from the equestrian order and from military service. Augustus maintained these barriers. He enrolled freedmen in the *vigiles*, but though organized on military lines the *vigiles* were not soldiers. It was only in the crises of the Pannonian revolt and the Varian disaster that he enrolled freedmen in the army, not in the legions but in special cohorts. He seems also to have excluded freedmen from municipal office and membership of town councils, or at any rate enforced their exclusion more rigorously, and finally he appears to have deprived them of their votes—freedmen are no longer enrolled in the tribes.

He was not, however, hostile to wealthy and public-spirited freedmen gaining some social recognition. He must at least have sanctioned the institution in many Italian towns of *seviri Augustales*, an annual board of six freedmen who conducted the cult of the *Lares Augusti*, and in return for this honour were expected to give games and contribute liberally to local amenities. An inscription from the municipality of Veii in honour of one of his own freedmen shows how high such a man might rise in the social scale:

It was unanimously resolved that until a decree could be drafted it should in the meanwhile by the resolution of all present be granted to Gaius Julius Gelos, freedman of the divine Augustus, who has at all times not only aided the municipality of Veii by his advice and influence, but also desired that games be celebrated at his expense by his son; that the highly deserved honour be decreed to him, that he should be deemed to be an *Augustalis* as if he had held that office, and that he should be allowed at all spectacles in our municipality to sit among the *Augustales* on his own seat, and to be present with the members of the city council at all public banquets (Ehrenberg & Jones, *Documents* 333).

At Rome Augustus appears to distinguish two definitions of the plebs. There was in the first place the *plebs Romana* or *plebs frumentaria*. These were the persons entitled to the free corn ration. They had risen to 320,000 in the late Republic, but had been reduced to 150,000 by Caesar, under whose regulations there was a fixed maximum of tickets, and as their holders died their tickets were issued to new applicants by lot. Nevertheless the numbers of the *plebs frumentaria* had apparently risen again to close on 250,000 in the earlier part of Augustus' reign. In 2 B.C. he cut down their number to 200,000. Augustus also speaks of the *plebs urbana*, which numbered 320,000. These are perhaps all citizens resident in Rome.

The Roman plebs had often been turbulent in the later Republic, but very few riots or demonstrations are heard of under Augustus except in 23–19 B.C., when there was a protest against his resigning the consulship. This may be partly due to improved policing. From an early date Augustus kept three praetorian cohorts of 1000 men each in the city; these eventually seem to have become the urban cohorts which the prefect of the city commanded. They were available for crushing major disorders. For everyday police duties Augustus in 8 B.C. divided Rome into 265 *vici* or wards, in each of which four *vicomagistri* were annually appointed from among the inhabitants. From A.D. 6 there were also the seven cohorts of *vigiles*, who on their nightly patrols not only detected and extinguished fires but arrested burglars. But the quiescence of the plebs was probably due more to better living conditions. *Panem et circenses* were, as Juvenal was later to say, the major interests of the plebs, and these were well supplied by Augustus. No more famines are heard of until A.D. 6, after which he entrusted the management of the corn supply to an equestrian prefect on whose efficiency he could rely. He gave numerous games, as he proudly records in the *Res Gestae*, three gladiatorial shows in his own name and five in those of his sons and grandsons, two shows of athletes in his own name and a third in that of his sons, twenty-six wild beast shows, a sea fight in an artificial basin, in which thirty full sized warships and many smaller craft fought, and four ordinary games, theatrical shows and chariot races, in his own name, and twenty-three in those of other magistrates. He also gave a considerable number of *congiaria*, 400 sesterces in 29, 24, and 12 B.C. to the urban plebs, and in 2 B.C. to the *plebs frumentaria*.

From the figures which Augustus gives it would appear that between a third and a quarter of the urban proletariat received no assistance from the state, and had to work to support themselves and their families. But even the lucky 250,000 or 200,000 who drew the free corn ration could not be idle, as Augustus recognized, when he planned to distribute the grain three times a year instead of monthly, to prevent the plebs being called away from their business too often. The ration was five *modii* a month, which would just furnish enough bread for a man and his wife. There was no surplus for children, and nothing for other food or for clothes or for rent. All citizens had to work to live. Many were small shopkeepers and craftsmen, but there was no large-scale industry in Rome except the building industry. Augustus' great programme of public works must have been the salvation of the urban plebs, giving them steady employment throughout the reign.

Augustus seems to have regarded the Roman plebs with the same contemptuous indulgence as most upper class Romans. He made no attempt to carry on his adoptive father's radical policy of sending them out to colonies overseas—Caesar is said to have thus given a new start in life to 80,000 —but kept them quiet with games and money distributions.

The towns of Italy flourished greatly under Augustus, to judge by their buildings and inscriptions. Strabo tells us that at Patavium no fewer than 500 *equites* (in the sense of persons owning 400,000 sesterces or more) were registered in one of Augustus' censuses.

The *plebs rustica*, the peasants of Italy, had for a century been subject to periodic unrest. Their demands were allotments of land and latterly remission of debt. Peasant families were too prolific, the family holding was split up between the children in each generation until it was no longer viable, the poverty stricken owners fell into debt, and eventually the moneylender, often a neighbouring landlord, foreclosed. This unrest stops abruptly with Augustus' reign. The reason must be the vast settlements of veterans—who were almost all poor or landless peasants—first by Caesar in his consulship and his dictatorship, then by Octavian after Philippi and after Actium (when 120,000 settled) and again by Augustus in 14 B.C. The majority seem to have been settled in Italy, but large numbers were planted in the provinces, easing the population pressure.

As a result of these huge settlements, many large estates cultivated by slaves must have been broken up into peasant allotments, and the land hunger of the *plebs rustica* must have been appeased for some time. Throughout the reign moreover superfluous members of peasant families could and did join the army, with the certainty of acquiring a piece of land—not necessarily in Italy—or enough money to buy one, if he survived for twenty years.

Apart from this revolutionary measure, which was a by-product of political and military exigencies, Augustus seems to have done little or nothing to encourage agriculture. We are told by Suetonius (*Augustus* 42, 3) that after the great famine of A.D. 6 Augustus wrote 'that he had the impulse to abolish the public distributions of corn permanently, because agriculture was declining owing to confidence in them'. His economics were probably wrong. Arable farming was being superseded by more profitable forms of agriculture, vines and olives, particularly in the areas within reach of Rome. The transport of corn to Rome was very heavy from the remoter parts of Italy. Land transport was prohibitively dear, and the sea voyage from Cisalpine Gaul, the only large arable area, was longer and more dangerous than from Sicily, Sardinia and Africa. It is unlikely that much Italian corn ever reached the Roman market, and the government import of corn from overseas can have done little harm to Italian farmers.

Augustus abandoned his impulse from political and not from economic reasons; the distributions, he reflected, would certainly be restored some day from ambition. All he did was

142

to manage the business so as to take as much account of the farmers and merchants as of the people. This presumably means that he instructed the *praefectus annonae* to buy Italian corn even if dearer than the provincial. This was the sum total of what Augustus did for Italian agriculture.

Religion

THE lower classes, so far as we can tell, continued in this period to worship the gods with simple faith. At any rate they made sacrifices to them, celebrated their feasts, and most significant of all, made vows to them in times of distress or danger and paid these vows if they were saved. In the Italian countryside the peasants worshipped the old traditional gods of the land. In Rome there was a mixture of cults. The immigrants, slave and free, who formed a large percentage of the population, naturally tended to cling to the gods of their various homelands. Some of these, like Serapis and Isis, attracted indigenous Romans.

The upper classes had since the early second century B.C. been tending to become more and more agnostic. The more serious minded among them followed one of the Greek philosophical schools. At Athens the Academic and Peripatetic schools still expounded and developed the teaching of Plato and Aristotle, and some few Roman nobles of intellectual tastes followed them; Cicero was an Academic. The ancient doctrines of Pythagoras were revived in the first century B.C., and Nigidius Figulus, a friend of Cicero who was praetor in 58 B.C. was a leader in the revival. There were Cynics at this period, but as they taught extreme asceticism and an ostentatious contempt for convention, it is unlikely that they converted senators. A more popular sect was the Sceptics, who maintained that there was no knowledge in the strict sense except of sense perceptions. For the practical purposes of life, however, they were prepared to accept propositions which were probable and to follow moral rules which were reasonable. Their adherents included Gaius Aurelius Cotta, consul in 75 B.C. In Cicero's day Epicureanism found an ardent exponent in Lucretius, who in his great poem, *De rerum natura*, relentlessly expounded the atomic theory on which it was based, and preached that men need have no fear of the supernatural; the gods were highly rarefied beings living a life of pleasure in interstellar space and took no interest in mankind, and the soul consisted of very fine atoms which were dispersed on death, so that there was no possibility of punishment beyond the grave. The wise man should lead a life of pleasure, by which was meant not women and wine, but tranquil intercourse with a small circle of friends. It was not a very suitable doctrine for an ambitious nobleman, but was nevertheless followed by Caesar's father-in-law, Calpurnius Piso, consul in 58 B.C. A more typical Epicurean was Horace.

The sect which appealed most strongly to the Roman aristocracy was Stoicism, as remodelled by Posidonius of Apamea, whose lectures Cicero heard at Rhodes in 78 B.C. The theoretical basis of its doctrine was that the universe was a living being, animated and ruled by a divine ethereal fire, which was identical with Reason. This fire enclosed the spherical universe, but it also interpenetrated it; each man's soul was a spark of this fire. The only good was virtue, which was to live 'according to nature', that is to accept whatever the divine fate or providence sent. This was possible for the wise man because a man's soul was derived from the same divine fire which guided the world. The commonly accepted good things, such as health and wealth, were indifferent, and the wise man was not troubled by their loss. In the troublous times of the late Republic this doctrine solaced many resolute men, faced with the loss of everything which they valued. The two great champions of the fallen Republic, Cato and Brutus, were Stoics.

These noble Roman philosophers were not of course professionals, and on the whole took little interest in the epistemological and cosmological arguments on which the various philosophies were based. They were indeed quite capable of taking one doctrine from one school and one from another even when incompatible; Cato, the Stoic, spent his last hours before his suicide in reading Plato's *Phaedo*. What they wanted was an intellectually respectable theory of the universe which would justify a satisfying code of conduct.

The philosophical schools were compatible with acceptance of, and even a belief in, the traditional gods. The Epicureans, it is true, turned the gods into remote and ethereal figures which took no interest in men, but they admitted their existence and saw no objection to worshipping them. Posidonius made room for the gods in the Stoic cosmological scheme. Even Sceptics could be pious worshippers of the gods. Aurelius Cotta, who managed to be simultaneously a Sceptic and a *pontifex*, declared:

> I have never thought any of these religious rites worthy of contempt, and so I have convinced myself that Romulus and Numa laid the foundations of our state by instituting the auspices and sacrifices. Surely Rome could never have become so great without the highest propitiation of the immortal gods. You have, Balbus, what Cotta the *pontifex* thinks. Now give me to understand what you think. I should accept from you as a philosopher the theory of religion; but I ought to believe our ancestors even if no rational explanation is offered. (Cicero, *On the Nature of the Gods* III, 5–6).

Such a mixtures of conservatism and patriotism was a strong factor for the preservation of the old religion against rationalism.

Philosophy was also not incompatible with superstition— or what would today be called superstition. Omens and auguries were universally believed in, and are sedulously recorded in the historians of the day. Astrology was regarded as a science. Its technique of observation was genuinely scientific, and its basic presupposition was generally acceptable. For Stoics in particular, who believed in the sympathy of the whole universe, from the stars of the outer circle of the heavenly sphere to the souls of men, it was natural to believe that the movements of the stars were linked with men's lives on earth. The Roman government disliked astrology, like all forms of private divination, and periodically expelled *mathematici* or *Chaldaei*. But this was because enquiries into such questions as the death of an emperor might be politically dangerous, not because astrology was fraudulent—though of course some of its professors might be. So sensible a man as Tiberius, who was in general negligent of the gods, had an implicit faith in Thrasyllus, his favourite astrologer; but he was also superstitious about thunder.

Under the later Republic the government tended to neglect religion. This may have been partly due to the growing scepticism of the upper classes, but it was also part of the general inefficiency and negligence of the Senate, preoccupied as it was with political conflicts. If the temples were allowed to fall in disrepair, as they were, so were the roads and the aqueducts. During the civil wars there was a revulsion of feeling. Faced by the unending succession of wars, proscriptions, famines and yet more wars, people began to feel uneasily that the gods must be angered with the Roman people, whether for its moral delinquencies or for its neglect of their worship. Horace voices this feeling in a famous ode (III, 6):

> Though guiltless, Roman, you will pay for the sins of your ancestors, until you rebuild the temples and the crumbling shrines of the gods, and their statues foul with black smoke. You rule because you bear yourself lower than the gods; to this refer every beginning and every end. The neglected gods have given many ills to mourning Italy. Twice already have Monaeses and the hosts of Pacorus beaten off our attacks that lacked the auspices.

This was true enough, but to go on to say that the Dacian and Ethiopian had almost captured Rome is somewhat exaggerated. Augustus may have shared this feeling, or, if he did not, have felt the need of assuaging popular fears. Whichever was the case, he initiated a revival of the old religious cults of Rome. He boasts that he repaired eighty-two temples, most of which must have been shrines of obscure old divinities. He revived obsolescent cult fraternities, like the Arval Brothers and the *Sodales Titii*. Ancient ceremonies were renewed, such as the *Augurium Salutiis*. He took pains to keep up the number of Vestals and was regretfully compelled in A.D. 5 to admit daughters of freedmen, when the upper classes did not respond to his appeals. In 1 B.C. he at last induced a patrician to undertake the unpopular post of *flamen dialis*, with its tiresome taboos; it had been vacant since Sulla's dictatorship.

The revival of obsolete cults is unlikely to have done much to stimulate religion, though it must have made an emotional appeal to pious conservatives of the type of Aurelius Cotta,

147

the *pontifex*. The movement was rather patriotic, and intended to revive memories of the old Republic and to stimulate the revival of the old Republican virtues. The ode of Horace cited above continues:

> Generations fertile in guilt have befouled marriage and the family and the home. Disaster flowing from this spring flooded the country and its people.

There then follows a salacious description of the misconduct of young wives, ending

> Not from such parents sprang the warriors who stained the seas with Punic blood and slew Pyrrhus and mighty Antiochus and dread Hannibal.

This Roman emphasis might have been expected to have as its counterpart the suppression of alien cults, not of course among the provincials, who had always been allowed to worship their own gods, however beastly and barbarous, but among Roman citizens. Augustus had his likes and dislikes among foreign religions. He was himself initiated in the Eleusinian mysteries, and took pride in being thus able to judge (having dismissed his unititiate assessors) a case between the two priestly families which managed the mysteries. On the other hand he disapproved of the Druidic cult with its human sacrifices, and forbade Roman citizens to participate in it. The only Roman citizens likely to be concerned would be Gallic nobles who had received the citizenship, and this measure reveals one of the difficulties of maintaining a pure Roman cult. He also disliked the Egyptian religion, and when passing by Memphis refused to turn aside to pay his respects to the Apis bull. Here again he took measures against the Serapis and Isis cult, which had been percolating even to Rome itself in the late Republic: the triumvirs had in their first year of office even built—or proposed to build—an official temple to Serapis. In 28 B.C. Augustus forbade the worship of the Egyptian gods within the *pomoerium*, and in 21 B.C. Agrippa, finding that it had revived, strengthened the ban and extended it for one mile beyond the *pomoerium*.

Towards the Jews Augustus was generally favourable; they had able advocates in Herod and his eloquent minister

Nicolaus of Damascus. Agrippa offered a hecatomb in the temple when he visited Jerusalem in 16 B.C., and it must have been Augustus who made the standing arrangement that he offered a regular oblation to the temple, from which were defrayed the costs of sacrifices offered twice a day on behalf of the emperor and the Roman people. He and Agrippa were also active in protecting the religious rights of the Jewish communities of the Diaspora. It is evident that there was widespread antisemitism throughout the Greek East. We have a letter of Octavian, before he became Augustus, to Norbanus Flaccus, proconsul of Asia, and consequential letters from him to Sardis and Ephesus, two other letters to Ephesus from Agrippa and Iullus Antonius, the proconsul, a letter of Agrippa to Cyrene, and an edict of Augustus to the provincial assembly of Galatia. The last goes into some detail. The Jews are not only to be allowed to practise their cult without hindrance; they are to be allowed to collect and send money to Jerusalem; they are not to have writs served on them on the Sabbath; theft of their holy books or cult objects is to be punished as sacrilege. Most of the letters specify only freedom of cult and the right to send money to Jerusalem. This practice of the Jews evidentally caused very bitter feelings. Jews held no offices and performed no liturgies, and to add insult to injury sent abroad the money that they ought to have spent in the service of their cities of residence.

Augustus' unusual favour to the Jews seems to have waned in his later life, when Herod fell out of favour. He is said to have commended Gaius Caesar for refusing to turn aside on his journey to Egypt in A.D. 1 to make an offering at the new Jewish temple. There is however no indication that Jewish privileges were not maintained.

Augustus' temples were not all antiquarian. He built a temple to his deified father, and another to Mars Ultor, which he had vowed to Mars if he killed all Caesar's murderers. This temple became the main centre for military affairs; the Senate met there to debate peace and war, commanders started from it for their campaigns, victors returned there and deposited in it their triumphal robes. His other main temple was originally vowed to Apollo in 36 B.C. when part of his house on the Palatine was struck by lightning, but rebuilt with greater splendour after 30 B.C., in honour of Apollo of Actium. It was later furnished with porticoes and two libraries, Greek and Latin. All these temples in one way or another glorify Augustus and his divine father. Agrippa added to the group by building the Pantheon, dedicated to Mars and Venus, the divine ancestors of the Julian family.

A problem which greatly exercised Augustus was his own worship. The Greek inhabitants of the eastern provinces were used to worshipping kings, and when they came under the Republican rule of Rome worshipped proconsuls, expensive though it was to build a temple a year. When a supreme head of the Empire appeared and he brought peace after the civil wars there was an irresistible urge to express their respect and gratitude in worship. It would seem that the sentiments of the Roman plebs and the Italian cities were not very different, though less ebullient. After the defeat of Sextus Pompeius and the restoration of peace and plenty in Italy, the cities of Italy set up Augustus' statue with those of the gods in their temples.

The Roman upper class were thus quite used to being worshipped by provincials, and indeed expected it, but they strongly resented any suggestion that they should worship one of their colleagues, or indeed that any Roman citizen should do so. Julius Caesar had added to his unpopularity by accepting official Roman worship, not that it was regarded as blasphemous, but ridiculous and pretentious, and savouring of regal pride.

Whether because he wished to avoid such odium, or because he had a genuine distaste for an un-Roman and oriental practice, Augustus was very cautious in accepting divine honours. It presumably pleased him when Horace declared—in a discreet future tense—that Augustus would recline between Pollux and Hercules and sip his nectar; but poetry was a different matter from cult. When after Actium the Greek inhabitants of Bithynia and Asia asked his leave to establish his cult at a provincial level, he replied that they must couple the goddess Roma with himself; and when the Roman residents of the two provinces made the same request, he refused, telling them to worship Roma and the deified Julius.

Seeing that provincial worship of proconsuls had been normal, this was very cautious, and the distinction between Greeks, who may worship him, and Romans, who may not, is marked.

These cults were maintained by provincial assemblies, consisting of delegates from all the cities, which met annually at the temple of Rome and Augustus to hold a festival, accompanied by games. To manage the festival they elected an annual high priest of the province, who usually covered most of the cost. The provincial high priesthood, held by the most distinguished and wealthiest members of the local aristocracy, became the highest honour which a provincial could hold, and the cult became a means of attaching the provincial notables to the Empire and its head.

Similar cults were founded in most of the eastern provinces. They did not always conform strictly to provincial boundaries—the Galatian tribes for instance, which had little in common with the other cities of the province of Galatia, had their separate organizations. Not all were dedicated to Rome and Augustus; Cyprus worshipped Augustus alone. Egypt was an exception. In the old Egyptian cult, conducted in the ancient temples, Augustus was Pharaoh and therefore *ex officio* a god; in the Greek cult he had temples in various cities and towns, but there was no provincial organization.

Augustus evidently came to see the value of the imperial cult in focusing and stimulating loyalty to Rome and to himself, for he seems to have promoted it in western provinces where there was no tradition of ruler worship. In 12 B.C. Drusus convened a conference of representatives of the sixty tribes of Gallia Comata at the confluence of the Rhone and the Saone near Lugdunum, and they elected as first high-priest of the three provinces an Aeduan who had received the Roman citizenship, Gaius Julius Vercundaris Dubius. Two years later the altar of Rome and Augustus, a splendid marble structure adorned with statues of the sixty tribes, was consecrated by Drusus. In 2 B.C. Domitius Ahenobarbus, legate of Germany, built an altar on the Elbe to serve the prospective province of Germany. Before A.D. 9 there was another altar for the Germans at the town of the Ubii, a German tribe on the west bank of the Rhine; it perhaps replaced Ahenobarbus' rather exposed shrine. There was an altar at Tarraco for Spain and probably another for Lusitania. Somewhat oddly Gallia Narbonensis and Africa did not institute provincial cults until two generations later. This can hardly have been from lack of loyalty, and is perhaps another example of Augustus' extreme caution. For these provinces contained a large number of Roman colonies and *municipia*, whose position would cause embarrassment. It would be churlish for them to opt out of the provincial organization, but for Roman towns to worship Augustus might excite hostile comment.

The provincial cults were semi-official and required imperial sanction. Municipal cults seem to have been little controlled, though it was normal for a city to ask the object of the proposed cult his or her permission. Large numbers of cities both in the East and the West instituted cults not only of Augustus but all the members of his family, Livia, Julia, Tiberius, Drusus, Gaius, Lucius and occasionally Agrippa. Roman towns were generally more guarded in the expression of their worship; the colonies of Carthage and Corinth worshipped the *gens Augusta*. But the *municipium* of Stobi in Macedonia spoke quite frankly of the god Caesar Augustus. Even in Italy itself a number of cities, including Puteoli and Pompeii, built temples to Augustus. In Rome itself the lower orders were allowed to worship the *genius* of Augustus at the Lares Compitales, the shrines of the city wards now renamed Lares Augusti, but all overt worship of the emperor was banned.

Literature and the Arts

AUGUSTUS could claim some credit for the Augustan age of Latin literature. According to Suetonius (*Augustus* 89, 3), 'He fostered the talent of his age in every way. He listened to recitations kindly and patiently, not only of poetry and history, but also speeches and dialogues.' These words suggest that Augustus regarded his patronage of literature as a tedious duty. Much of what he had to listen to may well have been boring, especially the speeches and dialogues, but other evidence suggests that he had not much literary appreciation. As a young man he studied rhetoric sedulously—he continued his daily exercises in reading, writing and declamation even in the campaign of Mutina—and he developed a quite pleasant unadorned style; but he never acquired facility, always preparing his public speeches carefully beforehand, and even writing a script for important conversations with his own wife. Though as a young man he was taught by Apollodorus of Pergamum, he never got far in Greek. He wrote his Greek speeches in Latin and had them translated. But he enjoyed Greek poetry and drama, and he patronized some Greek philosophers. Arius of Alexandria and Athenodorus of Tarsus accompanied him in 30 B.C. to the East. On the latter he bestowed the government of Tarsus with dictatorial powers, with the mission of reforming its government from the democratic licence of Antonian days. When he spared the Alexandrians any penalty he told them that they owed it to Serapis, Alexander the Great and their fellow citizen Arius.

It may be suspected that Augustus was not interested in philosophy, but liked to have eminent philosophers in his entourage as domestic chaplains. In the authors that he read, Suetonius tells us, what he chiefly looked for were precepts and examples useful for public or private life. He used to keep a file of notable passages, and sent appropriate texts

to urban magistrates, provincial governors and army commanders as occasion demanded.

Be that as it may, Augustus certainly took an active interest
in a number of the younger historians and poets. Livy seems
to have become quite an intimate friend of the family, and
he encouraged young Claudius to write history too. Augustus
gave high promotion to the poet Cornelius Gallus, and offered
Horace the post of private secretary. Virgil he knew well
and took a great interest in the progress of the *Aeneid*.

It was his friend Maecenas, however, who took the lead in
patronizing young poets, and introduced them to Augustus.
At the very beginning of the triumvirate he collected a notable
group of very various origins. Propertius came from Umbria
and was of equestrian rank. Cornelius Gallus, also of equestrian rank, came from Gallia Narbonensis, from the Roman
settlement of Forum Iulii. Virgil was of humbler origin,
son of a small farmer in the territory of Mantua, but had
received a good education. His farm was confiscated for the
settlement of veterans after Philippi, but restored to him
through the interest of Asinius Pollio, the historian, who was
a patron of letters. Horace was the humblest of all, son of a
freedman. His father had however given him an excellent
education, finally sending him to Athens. While he was a
student there Brutus took over Macedonia, and with youthful
patriotic fervour Horace obtained a commission as military
tribune and fought on the wrong side at Philippi. Returning
to Rome he had enough money left to buy the post of *scriba
quaestorius* (these posts were regularly saleable). However,
he was not obliged to fulfil the tedious duties of a treasury
clerk for long: he got to know Virgil and his friend Varius
Rufus, and so was introduced to Maecenas.

Ovid was a younger man. He came from an equestrian
family of the Paeligni. His father was ambitious, wanting
him to go into politics, and he got as far as the vigintivirate.
His only love, however, was poetry, and he abandoned his
broad stripe. He was a friend of Horace and Propertius,
but Virgil died before he had got to know him. With these
friends, it may be presumed that he belonged to Maecenas'
circle, as did perhaps his great friend Macer.

Maecenas did not attract all the poets of the day into his

orbit. Messala Corvinus the historian patronized another group, including Tibullus, Sulpicius and the poet Tibullus called by the pseudonym of Lygdamus.

Most of the historians were nobles, like Asinius Pollio and Messala Corvinus, or at any rate senators, like Velleius Paterculus and Cremutius Cordus. Livy was of middle class origin from Patavium in Cisalpine Gaul—Asinius Pollio detected Patavinitas in Livy's Latin—and was the only historian of the day to receive Augustus' patronage.

There were also Greek historians who wrote under Augustus. Nicolaus of Damascus wrote a Universal History; he met Augustus several times as Herod's diplomatic agent, and he also wrote a biography of Augustus, but Herod was his patron. Diodorus of Agyrium in Sicily wrote another Universal History. It is not surprising that Augustus took no interest in these two works, which were mostly concerned with Oriental and Greek history, but it is strange that he ignored Dionysius of Halicarnassus, who came to Rome the year after Actium, and wrote on Roman Antiquities beginning with the foundation of the city and going down to the first Punic war. It is an enormous work on a much larger scale than Livy's, and replete with interminable speeches, but it is very learned, and full of the precepts and examples that Augustus loved.

Augustus did not impose any political or moral censorship on authors, nor was he very exacting in pressing them to glorify himself and his regime. The poets of the age were mostly admirers and imitators of the Alexandrian school, and wrote by preference love poetry or mythological, pastoral or didactic verse. Cornelius Gallus was famous for his pastoral and love poetry. Propertius wrote two poems in praise of Augustus, and six on ancient Roman cults, which may have been intended to please him; the rest of his work is almost entirely love poetry. Macer wrote learned didactic poems. Varius Rufus wrote one epic in praise of Augustus; his remaining epics, his elegies and his tragedies had no references to the emperor or his policy. Horace wrote a few patriotic odes celebrating Augustus' conquests, actual or anticipated (which included Parthia and Britain), and supporting his moral and religious reforms. But the great bulk of his work, satire, literary criticism, love poetry and occasional verses, is purely personal.

Ovid spent about twenty-five years of his life writing erotic and mythological verse, some of which, as he must have very well known, was likely to cause Augustus the gravest displeasure. He then at last began to write the *Fasti*, a versified calendar of the festivals and anniversaries of the Roman state. This must obviously have been intended as a contribution to the Augustan religious reforms, but it came too late. Ovid had only half finished it when Augustus relegated him without trial to Tomi in Moesia. One reason is said to have been a poem, the *Ars Amatoria*, the other a crime or misdemeanour which Ovid never reveals, but which he admitted to be serious. Augustus' action can hardly be called an exercise of literary censorship. The *Ars Amatoria* was an overt incitement to crime, adultery having been defined as criminal nearly twenty years before its publication. No action was taken against the book for nine years, and then only in conjunction with some other serious charge.

Virgil started with pastoral verse in the fashion of the day, and went on to a didactic poem. Maecenas is said to have suggested the subject, agriculture, but it is most unlikely that it was chosen in order to promote Augustus' plans for the economic revival of Italy; so far as we know, Augustus had no such plans, and the *Georgics* are not, and were not intended to be, an agricultural manual. Didactic poetry was one of the contemporary vogues, and farming was congenial to Virgil's tastes. Nor is there any firm evidence that the *Aeneid* was dictated or suggested by Augustus. Virgil naturally aspired to write an epic, which was accounted the noblest poetic form: the question was what was to be the subject. In the third book of the *Georgics* Virgil announces that he is eager to go on to a nobler theme, the warlike achievements of Augustus. But if this suggestion came from Augustus, it was not pressed, and eventually Virgil wrote on a much more congenial theme. The Homeric model prescribed as subject a piece of mythological history. In the patriotic temper of the age it was natural that Virgil should choose an early Roman theme. He might perhaps have chosen Romulus, but Aeneas had the advantage of linking early Rome with the Trojan war. It was also true that Aeneas was the forefather of the Julian *gens*, but Virgil rarely makes explicit reference to this fact. The *Aeneid* undoubtedly gave great pleasure to Augustus, not merely for its allusions to himself and his adoptive family, but because it glorified Rome and praised the Roman virtues. But there can be no doubt that Virgil himself had a deep sense of the greatness of Rome and of the qualities which made her great.

With the exception of Velleius the historians were all Republicans who condemned Caesar and lauded his assassins, Brutus and Cassius. That was the line taken by Asinius Pollio and Messalla Corvinus and later by Cremutius Cordus, whose works were burned as treasonable under Tiberius. Livy was so strong a supporter of Pompeius Magnus against Caesar that Augustus called him a Pompeian. Relations were nevertheless very friendly between them, and Augustus fully appreciated Livy's glorification of the old Republican virtues.

Augustus was a great patron of art in as far as he commissioned many buildings and paid lavishly for them out of his private means. In the *Res Gestae* he gives a long list of the monuments which he restored, rebuilt or erected for the first time.

On the Capitol he restored the great temple of Jupiter, Juno and Minerva 'at great expense', rebuilt the old temple of Jupiter Feretrius where Romulus' *spolia opima* were dedicated, and built, in fulfilment of a vow—he narrowly escaped being struck by lightning in Spain—a new temple of Jupiter Tonans. In the Forum he built a new senate house (*curia*), with its annex, the Chalcidicum, and new rostra. He rebuilt his adoptive father's Basilica Julia, which had been burnt down, and the old Basilica Aemilia, and erected nearby a magnificent new temple to his deified father. Other temples at this end of the Forum were rebuilt by his family and friends. Munatius Plancus rebuilt the temple of Saturn, the treasury of the Roman state, Tiberius the temples of Concord and Castor. The *regia*, the official residence of the *pontifex maximus*, was rebuilt by Domitius Calvinus. At the other end of the Forum Augustus rebuilt the ancient shrine of the Lares and Penates of the Roman state.

Even after the addition of the Forum Julium, the Forum

remained very congested. Augustus built a third Forum, at right angles to his father's, and assigned it to the *iudicia publica* and the sortition of jurors for them. The Forum was flanked by colonnades and two large *exedrae* and at the far end stood the temple of Mars Ultor, the avenger of Caesar.

The Palatine Hill, on which Augustus lived, was specially favoured. The principal monument was a vast new temple of Apollo, with flanking porticos and libraries. Augustus also rebuilt the old temple of the Great Mother, and converted the Lupercal, the cave in which Romulus and Remus had been suckled by the wolf, into an ornamental grotto. On the Quirinal he rebuilt the ancient temple of Quirinus, and on the Aventine three other ancient temples, that of Diana, dedicated during the second Punic war, that of Juno Regina, vowed to that goddess by Camillus during the siege of Veii, and that of Jupiter Libertas. Lucius Cornificius rebuilt another even more ancient temple of Diana on the Palatine.

The main building area was the wide space between the Via Flaminia and the river north and east of the Capitol, including the Campus Martius. There had been some scattered monuments already erected on the southern side of it during the Republic. There was the Circus Flaminius, built by the censor of 220 B.C.; the Porticus Octavia, the work of a putative ancestor of Augustus, consul in 165 B.C., and therefore rebuilt by him; the Porticus Metelli, built in 149 B.C. and rebuilt in honour of Octavia and renamed the Porticus Octaviae; finally the great theatre of Pompeius, which Augustus restored 'at great expense'. There was, however, still plenty of space, and not only Augustus but many of the great men of the day contributed to filling it.

In the extreme north Augustus built his huge mausoleum, a strange circular building with a steep conical roof. In the extreme south he erected a theatre which he dedicated to Marcellus. This area was the main field for Agrippa, who completed Julius Caesar's Saepta Iulia in the Campus Martius, and built the Porticus Argonautarum to celebrate his naval victories, another portico to display his great map of the Empire, and the Pantheon and behind it a great bath, which set the pattern for the later imperial *thermae*. Domitius Ahenobarbus, Gaius Silius and Marcius Philippus built temples to Neptune, Apollo and Hercules of the Muses. More ambitious, Cornelius Balbus built a theatre and Statilius Taurus an amphitheatre.

Though we know what buildings Augustus erected, we have no means of telling how much interest he took in them, or how far he influenced their plans and style. He boasted, we are told, that he had found Rome a city of brick and left it one of marble (Suetonius, *Augustus* 28, 3). This is substantially true, for marble was little used under the Republic, and became almost invariable in Augustus' reign. The remark tells us little, however, except that Augustus had a taste for the magnificent and was prepared to pay for it. We do not know even the names of his architects, much less how he chose them and where they came from. Probably most of them were Greeks—in the sense of men from the eastern provinces— because there were few competent Italians for the kind of thing which Augustus evidently wanted, whereas good Greek architects abounded. This hypothesis is confirmed by the style of the buildings and sculptures, which become distinctly more Hellenistic in Augustus' reign.

It is difficult to appreciate the architectural achievement of the Augustan age; so few buildings survive. Several of Augustus' monuments were burnt down in the first, second and third centuries and rebuilt on new lines. From the fourth century onwards all Roman temples were closed, and gradually pulled to pieces to provide columns and architraves for the new Christian basilicas, and Augustus' marble temples provided the best material for them. Of only one Augustan building does enough survive to make it easy to picture the whole, the theatre of Marcellus. It is an elegant and well-proportioned building, built on the formula established in the post-Sullan era, three superposed arcades, framed with columns and architraves of the three orders, Doric, Ionic, and Corinthian. There are scantier remains of what was evidently a finer monument, the temple of Mars Ultor and the Forum Augusti in which it stood. Here there survives much of the podium of the temple, on which four tall slender fluted Corinthian columns still stand carrying their architraves; also most of the surrounding wall of the eastern half of the Forum. One is helped in visualizing the temple by a miniature relief of its west front, showing the lofty flight of steps, the eight columns of the portico and its sculptured pediment with bold acroteria in the form of Victories. This clearly was a very striking temple, imposing for its height, which must have dominated the Forum. The rather peculiar shape of the Forum may be partly due to the fact that Augustus was unable to persuade some of the adjacent landowners to sell and refused to use any compulsory powers. If so Augustus' architects got round the difficulty admirably. The main body of the Forum is a rectangle flanked by wide colonnaded aisles, but on either side of the temple these aisles open into large semicircular *exedrae*, giving more space to the temple which might otherwise have been cramped.

There are some minor Augustan monuments in Italy, but they are not the work of Augustus himself, and do not look as if they were built by his architects. The Senate and people of Rome put up at Arimium a singularly inept arch, which has a pediment which is too short, so that it does not rest on the columns. Julius Cottius, son of King Donnus and prefect of a group of Alpine tribes, put up a simple but elegant arch at Segusio. On the other side of the Alps the Senate and people of Rome erected a curious trophy, now reconstructed, to celebrate Augustus' conquest of the Alpine tribes. It consisted of a square podium, on which stands a cylindrical drum, probably capped by a pyramid carrying a trophy or a statue of Augustus.

Considerably more sculpture survives. The most famous monument is perhaps the Ara Pacis, erected by the Senate and people to celebrate the pacification of Gaul and Spain; it was voted in 13 B.C. but not finished until 9 B.C. What survives, or rather has been reconstructed, is the square enclosure with doorways in the eastern and western sides, within which the actual altar stood. The exteriors of the walls are carved with reliefs, allegorical figures of Rome and Italy (?) flanking the east door, mythological scenes of Aeneas and Romulus and Remus the west. The south wall shows Augustus, attended by lictors, the Vestal Virgins and the priestly colleges, making a libation; next follow the family and close relations of Augustus. On the north there is a long procession of senators, followed by a few representatives of the Roman people. The

reliefs have a certain severity but the carving is of great deli-
cacy; they are rightly esteemed as one of the masterpieces of
Roman art. The themes naturally reflect the ideals of the
new regime. The revival of the old religion is represented in
the colleges of priests, the restored Senate dominates one wall.
Flanking Romulus the founder of Rome—whose name
Augustus wanted to take—is Aeneas, the ancestor of the
gens Iulia. Perhaps the most significant sign of the times
is a large group of Augustus' relatives including some children—these last one of the most charming features of the
reliefs.

We have numerous portraits of Augustus and of his family.
The most famous statue is that found in Livia's villa *ad
Gallinas* near the ninth milestone of the Flaminian Way,
commonly called the Augustus of Primo Porta from the name
of the modern village on the site. It is a full length statue
showing Augustus in military attire. The reliefs on the breast-
plate show Caelus, Sol driving his chariot and Aurora, believed to symbolize the dawn of a new age for the Empire, and
among other figures below is a Parthian handing over standards to Mars. The statue must have been carved soon after
20 B.C., and shows Augustus in his middle forties. One may
wonder whether Livia liked to remember her husband thus,
or whether she relegated it to a suburban villa which she
never visited. This villa incidentally possesses one of the most
delightful sets of wall-paintings that has survived from anti-
quity. All four walls of a large room are painted with what is
almost a *trompe d'œil*, depicting a flower bed behind a low
trellis and beyond a shrubbery which is also a bird sanctuary.

One work of the minor arts deserves mention, the Gemmea
Augustea. It is a cameo, carved from sardonyx, with the
figures in white on a dark background. In the centre Rome
and Augustus are seated side by side on a wide throne. Above
Augustus is capricorn, his zodiacal sign, and beneath him the
eagle of Jupiter. On the right are Terra Mater with a cornu-
copia of plenty and two other allegorical figures, one of which
is crowning Augustus with the *corona civica*, which the Senate
voted to him in 27 B.C. On the left Tiberius, attended by a
Victory, descends from a chariot, whose horses are led by a
young man, probably either Germanicus or Gaius Caesar,

according to whether the gem was cut for Tiberius' triumph of 7 B.C. or A.D. 12. Below this group are Roman soldiers erecting a trophy and dragging barbarian prisoners by the hair.

15

Augustus

AUGUSTUS' seal was a sphinx, and he is indeed an enigmatic figure, whom some have detested and others extravagantly admired. It is all the more difficult to assess his character as most of the evidence is biased. For his career before Actium some of the material clearly comes from hostile propaganda of Republicans and Antonians; one can see the story of the Sacrifice of Perusia becoming more sensational. After Actium we have very little that is not laudatory, and even Tacitus can only make dark hints of a sinister background.

It cannot be denied that as a young man he was ruthless and unscrupulous. It can be urged in his excuse that he was in a very vulnerable position, and that his adversaries were also unscrupulous and ruthless. If he double-crossed Cicero and the Republicans after the battle of Mutina, they were intending to double-cross him directly Antonius was eliminated. If he did not keep his agreements with Antonius and sent him no legions from Italy, Antonius never sent to Augustus any of the money that he had engaged to send from the eastern provinces.

Augustus was ruthless even after Actium, executing not only Turullius and Cassius of Parma, the last surviving assassins of Caesar, which may have seemed a sacred duty, but Antonius' elder son, Antullus; Curio, who had supported Caesar as tribune of the plebs, but quarrelled with his adoptive son; the two brothers Aquilius Florus; Canidius Crassus, who had commanded the Antonian infantry at Actium; and Ptolemy Caesar, his own brother by adoption. Some of these executions can be called political necessities, but others can hardly be so justified. Augustus' boast in the *Res Gestae* (3), 'Victorious I spared all citizens who asked for pardon', is thus not strictly true. But thereafter he seems to have lived up to his much advertised virtue of clemency, for which (with his courage, justice and piety) the Senate presented him with a golden shield.

AUGUSTUS

Augustus must have had some sterling qualities to win and keep the devoted loyalty of a number of friends. The most famous examples are Agrippa and Maecenas. Agrippa was a faithful friend from before Caesar's murder to his own death in 12 B.C. and during those thirty-two years there is never a hint of a quarrel. Augustus was estranged from Maecenas in 23 B.C., but was apparently soon reconciled; their friendship lasted over fifty years. Both left their fortunes to Augustus. Augustus' other supporters are mostly known to us only from their careers, but two at least were his intimate friends. In a chatty letter to Tiberius, preserved by Suetonius, Augustus describes Silius Nerva, proconsul of Illyricum and later legate of Spain, and Vinicius, a new man who had a long military career, coming to dinner with him and having a prolonged and exciting dicing party.

We know nothing of his relations with his first three wives, all married for political reasons, except that he divorced Scribonia because he was 'tired of the perversity of her character' (Suetonius, *Augustus* 62, 2). His love match with Livia was a conspicuous success, despite her failure to produce a much desired heir, and they lived together happily for over fifty years: Augustus was not strictly faithful to her, but this was not expected of Roman husbands. He appears to have been too strict with his daughter Julia, making her occupy her leisure hours in spinning and weaving in the antique Roman fashion. He also married her without any regard to her feelings or those of her successive husbands to politically useful persons, the young Marcellus, the very elderly Agrippa, and Tiberius, who loved his first wife and disliked Julia. It is not surprising that Julia went off the rails. By contrast he seems to have spoilt his adoptive sons, Gaius and Lucius. Tiberius was a difficult character, proud and reserved, and Augustus was not altogether successful in handling him. He led him to believe that he was the destined heir, granting him special privileges as early as 24 B.C., constantly employing him as his legate on important wars and missions, giving him the pro-consular *imperium*, and finally the tribunician power in 6 B.C. Tiberius was not unnaturally bitterly aggrieved when he saw the exaggerated honours bestowed on Gaius and Lucius, and retired in dudgeon to Rhodes. The quarrel was not healed until both Gaius and Lucius were dead, and it was Augustus who kept it up when Tiberius was willing to be reconciled with him. This period, however, is not typical of their relations. Suetonius has preserved some scraps of letters from Augustus to Tiberius which reveal a very relaxed and intimate relationship between them.

Another letter from Augustus to Livia (Suetonius, *Claudius* 4), discussing the future of her backward grandson Claudius, reveals remarkable patience and indeed affection for a boy who was a great political embarrassment.

I have talked with Tiberius, as you told me, Livia, about what is to be done about your grandson Claudius at the games of Mars. We both agreed that we must decide once and for all what plan to follow about him. For if he is, if I may say so, really normal, why should we hesitate to advance him by the same stages as his brother? But if we feel that he is defective, both in body and mind, we must not give occasion for people who are in the habit of sneering and mocking at such things to deride both him and us. We shall be always hesitating without making a decision in principle if we debate on each occasion whether we think he can hold an office or not. For the moment, however, on the matter on which you asked my advice, we do not mind his presiding at the table of the priests at the games of Mars, if he will allow himself to be advised by the son of Silius, who is his kinsman, so that he may not do anything to attract stares and ridicule. We do not think he ought to watch the games from the imperial box, as he would be exposed to view in the front of the spectators. We do not think he ought to go to the Alban Mount or be in Rome at the Latin games. For why should not he be made prefect of the city, if he can follow his brother to the Mount?

And in another letter (Suetonius, *Claudius* 4):—

I shall ask the young Claudius to dinner every day while you are away, so that he may not dine alone with Sulpicius and Athenodorus. I wish he would pick out for himself more carefully and less casually someone whose manners and gait he will imitate. The poor boy is unhappy, for the nobility of his soul appears clearly enough in serious studies, where his mind is not astray.

Augustus was conservative, not to say old-fashioned, in his tastes. He made the women of his family spin and weave in the old-fashioned way, and actually wore the homespun that they produced. He tried to make people wear the antiquated toga, which had gone out except for formal occasions. Indignantly quoting Virgil's line, *Romanos rerum dominos gentemque togatam* (Romans, lords of the world, the toga-clad race), he instructed the aediles to turn people out of the Forum and its neighbourhood if not wearing togas (Suetonius, *Augustus* 45, 5). He revived old ceremonies and offices and cults, and banned new foreign gods from the city. His views on marriage were antiquated; he found them so well expressed by a censor of 131 B.C., Metellus Macedonicus, that he read aloud Metellus' speech on the subject to the Senate when introducing the *lex Julia de maritandis ordinibus*.

This encouragement of old-fashioned manners and customs had its political side, being intended to buttress the restored Republic, but there can be little doubt that Augustus valued them for their own sake. The restored Republic itself was a rather archaic revival. Augustus was probably expressing his real political sentiments when he said (of Cato):

> The man who does not wish to change the existing political order, is a good citizen and a good man (Macrobius, *Saturnalia* II, 4, 18).

But if Augustus was in many ways a conservative he was not afraid to innovate where efficiency and justice demanded it. He converted the ill-organized and ramshackle army of the Republic into the efficient professional force which successfully defended the frontiers for centuries. After the long squabbles of Republican days he established machinery for providing a regular discharge bounty for his soldiers. He set up for the first time a system of appeals, whereby discontented litigants could have their cases reviewed. He established an equitable system of taxation in place of arbitrary *stipendia* and the grossly oppressive tithe of the Republic. In the city of Rome he cleared up the muddle of the Republic and set up efficient departments to manage the municipal services.

Perhaps his greatest gift was his political tact. He evidently had a passion for efficiency, but he was careful not to offend public opinion by violent changes, but to work as far as possible within established forms. He was determined to rule the Empire, but he disguised his absolute powers in constitutional wrappings, and thus made them acceptable to the upper classes, and established a form of government which proved more or less stable for over two centuries.

16

The Sources

T HERE is one unique source for the career of Augustus, the record of his achievements which he wrote himself, and directed to be engraved on two bronze plaques outside his mausoleum. The bronze plaques have perished, but three loyal cities in Galatia, Ancyra, Apollonia and Antioch of Pisidia, inscribed copies of the document, or of the official Greek translation, on their temples, and of these copies sufficient has survived to make a complete reconstruction possible.

The *Res Gestae Divi Augusti*[1] do not profess to be an autobiography of Augustus nor a history of his reign. They are an extended obituary notice, and they depict Augustus as he wished to be remembered, as the great statesman and general, who had enacted wise laws; won many wars and added provinces to the Empire of the Roman people; contributed huge sums from his private fortune for public purposes; adorned Rome with temples and public buildings; amused the Roman plebs with magnificent games; distributed lavish *congiaria* and donatives to the people and the army; and finally been offered by a grateful Senate and people numerous honours, many of which he modestly refused.

It seems improbable that in a document that was to be publicly displayed Augustus made any statement that was obviously untrue, and as far as we can test his narrative it is accurate. But if he wrote the truth and nothing but the truth, he certainly did not write the whole truth. It would

[1] Text in Victor Ehrenberg and A. H. M. Jones, *Documents Illustrating the Reigns of Augustus and Tiberius* (2nd edition, Oxford and New York, Oxford University Press, 1963); text and translation in the Loeb series (Cambridge, Mass., Harvard University Press; London, Heinemann); text, translation and commentary in P. A. Brunt and J. M. Moore, *Res Gestae Divi Augusti, the Achievement of the Divine Augustus* (Oxford and New York, Oxford University Press, 1967).

be unreasonable to expect Augustus to give a plain unvarnished account of the way that he rose to power, but his allusions to that part of his life are highly disingenuous. He only twice alludes to civil wars; to say that he extinguished them and that, when he had won them, he spared all citizens who begged for pardon. He manages to avoid mentioning his opponents. Lepidus appears only as the anonymous person who usurped the office of *pontifex maximus* during a civil disturbance. The defeat of Sextus Pompeius is the suppression of a servile revolt whose leader is unnamed. The final struggle against Antonius is 'the war that I won at Actium'. In his foreign wars he never admits a failure or a defeat. Aelius Gallus' failure to conquer the Sabaeans becomes a victorious march into the heart of Arabia. The collapse of his attempts to impose a client king on Armenia in the last decade of his reign is passed over in silence. Not a word is said of the great Pannonian revolt or the Varian disaster, and the abandonment of the plan so long pursued to annex Germany up to the Elbe is ignored.

On constitutional affairs he is also disingenuous. He records with loving care every outward honour which he received, down to the inclusion of his name in the Salian hymn, and he proudly records his rejection of unconstitutional powers and offices. But he fails to mention that in 27 B.C. he received four huge provinces, or that these, with more added to them, were renewed at decennial or quinquennial intervals for the rest of his life. This omission makes one wonder whether Augustus has not quietly omitted to mention other important constitutional powers which others record.

There are many other inscriptions[1] besides the *Res Gestae* which add substantially to our knowledge. Most are honorific or funerary inscriptions of senators, *equites*, soldiers and imperial slaves or freedmen, setting out their careers. There are very many which illustrate the imperial cult. They are for the most part monotonous, but one decree of the province of Asia is remarkable for the messianic language in which it greets the good tidings of Augustus' appearance on earth: the substance of the decree is rather an anti-climax—Asia accepts the

[1] There is a selection in Ehrenberg and Jones, *op. cit.*

169

proposal of its proconsul that the highest honour it can offer to the god is to adopt the Julian calendar with Augustus' birthday as New Year's Day. There are a number of other longer texts, some of human interest, like the acts of the Ludi Saeculares which state that Quintus Horatius Flaccus composed the hymn, or one of the grandiloquent inscriptions which cost Cornelius Gallus his job and ultimately his life; others of high constitutional interest like the grant of Roman citizenship and other privileges by Octavian as triumvir to Seleucus of Rhosus, the oath of allegiance sworn by the Paphlagonians to Augustus in 3 B.C., the letter of Augustus to Cnidus, the letter of a proconsul of Asia to Chios, the edict of Augustus on the aqueduct of Venafrum, and above all Augustus' five edicts of Cyrene and the *senatus consultum* on trials for extortion which the last cites.

The papyri contain little of general interest except an edict of Octavian as triumvir, granting privileges to veterans. There are a number of other Augustan documents embedded in later writers. Josephus cites a number of edicts and letters of Augustus and Agrippa to various eastern cities confirming the privileges of the Jews. Frontinus in the historical introduction to his monograph on the aqueducts quotes *in extenso* a law and several *senatus consulta* passed in 11 B.C. when the *curatores aquarum* were instituted.[1]

The editor of Cicero's letters suppressed his correspondence with the young Octavian, but there survive in the other letters a number of vivid and illuminating glimpses of the young man; the picture given by the letters is strikingly different from that given in Cicero's speeches.[2] Some private letters of Augustus are quoted by Suetonius, who presumably found them in the files of his office when he served as *ab epistulis* to Hadrian.

[1] These are all in Ehrenberg and Jones, *op. cit.*, nos. 278–9, 302, 304–6, 309–10.

[2] The most convenient edition is R. Y. Tyrrell and L. C. Purser, *The Correspondence of Marcus Tullius Cicero* (London, 1899) where the relevant letters (with notes) are printed in chronological order in Vol. VII; translation in E. S. Shuckburgh, *Cicero, Letters; the whole extant correspondence in chronological order translated into English* (London, 1899).

THE SOURCES

The Augustan poets throw a good deal of light on Roman society, particularly its seamier side, and Horace in his odes refers to Augustus' military successes and anticipated conquests—the latter including Parthia and Britain—and advertises his programme of religious revival and moral reformation.

Augustus wrote his autobiography as far as the Cantabrian war, apparently on a considerable scale; it ran to thirteen books. Only about twenty scraps survive and they are mostly trivial. Agrippa also wrote an autobiography, of which only two or three snippets exist.[1] Nicolaus of Damascus, the court historian of Herod the Great, wrote a life of Augustus in Greek: only a few fragments survive, but two give vivid accounts of episodes in his early life.[2]

Nicolaus of Damascus also wrote a Universal History which came down to Herod's death in 4 B.C. It is lost, but Josephus' account of Herod's reign is largely based on it.[3] Strabo of Amaseia in Pontus wrote besides his surviving Geography a History. This has perished, but his Geography contains much contemporary history.[4] He was naturally familiar with eastern Asia Minor, where he gives up-to-date information on Pontus and Cappadocia, and he also visited Egypt as the guest of the prefect Aelius Gallus, and describes the new administrative system. He is also well informed on the new system in Spain, which he does not claim to have visited, and gives us the earliest account of the provincial set-up in 27 B.C.

A number of other historians told the story of their time in Latin. Asinius Polio,[5] a nobleman of independent political views and literary tastes—he was the friend and patron of Horace and Virgil—wrote a history of the decline and fall of the Republic, starting from 60 B.C. and including the proscriptions. Valerius Messalla Corvinus[6] also started as a

[1] Fragments in H. Peter, *Historicorum romanorum reliquiae* (Teubner, 1906, Vol. II, 54–65).

[2] Fragments in F. Jacoby, *Die Fragmente der griechischen Historiker* (Berlin, 1926, Vol. II, 90).

[3] Text and translation in the Loeb series.

[4] Text and translation in the Loeb series.

[5] Fragments in Peter, *op. cit.*, Vol. II, 67–70.

[6] Fragments in Peter, *op. cit.*, Vol. II, 65–7.

Republican—he fought with Brutus and Cassius at Philippi, but gave up the cause as hopeless and joined Antonius and a few years later shifted his allegiance to Octavian, whose colleague he was as consul in the year of Actium. He too was a patron of poets, notably of Tibullus, and wrote a history which included the battles of Philippi and Actium. Livy carried down his great history of Rome to 9 B.C., devoting no less than twenty books to the period from Caesar's murder. Only jejune epitomes survive.[1] Another senator, Cremutius Cordus,[2] was condemned for treason in A.D. 25 for his historical works. He evidently included the civil wars, since he praised Brutus and called Cassius the last of the Romans. He also described Augustus' first revision of the senatorial roll in 28 B.C. and probably covered all the reign; Augustus showed his broadmindedness by hearing the work—or a portion of it —recited to him.

Only one contemporary history of the reign has survived, that of Velleius Paterculus.[3] Velleius was a senator of Samnite origins, and evidently had a strong military bent. He must have served a number of years as military tribune, under Marcus Vinicius and Publius Silanus in Thrace and Macedonia, and then on the staff of Gaius Caesar, when he witnessed the meeting of Gaius and the Parthian king on the Euphrates in A.D. 2. Quaestor elect in the year of the Pannonian revolt (A.D. 6) he was ordered to march reinforcements to Tiberius, and served for a number of years as his legate in Pannonia. He became praetor in A.D. 15, one of the last group of Augustus' candidates and the first of Tiberius'.

His history is a very sketchy and naïve piece of work. It covers the whole history of Rome from the Trojan war to Tiberius' reign in two books, of which about half a book is devoted to Augustus' reign. He does however give a reasonably full account of the northern wars, in which he is chiefly interested. But perhaps his history is most useful in revealing the attitude to the restored Republic of a young man who had never known the old Republic or the civil wars. He manages to combine a great admiration of the old

[1] Text and translation in the Loeb series.
[2] Fragments in Peter, *op. cit.*, Vol. II, 87–90.
[3] Text and translation in the Loeb series.

Republic with an equally sincere admiration for the new regime.

Somewhat later Annaeus Seneca of Corduba, the father of Galleo, proconsul of Achaea, and of Seneca the philosopher, wrote a history which included the civil wars and went down to the death of Tiberius. Aufidius Bassus wrote under Tiberius and Claudius a history which began with Caesar's murder and continued after Tiberius' death. Servilius Nomianus, consul in A.D. 25, wrote a history whose scope is unknown. Finally the emperor Claudius began writing the history of the civil wars, but gave it up after completing two books, and began again with Actium, writing forty-one books, which must have covered Augustus' reign.[1]

It would be wearisome to continue a catalogue of secondary historians of whom little or nothing survives. This list will suffice to show that there was plenty of contemporary or near contemporary material for the later historians who have survived to draw upon. In the next century, fortunately for Augustus' posthumous fame, Tacitus began his Annals *ab excessu divi Augusti*; the sinister insinuations in the two chapters which he devotes to his achievements and character (*Annals* I) shows clearly enough how Augustus would have emerged. Suetonius' life of Augustus[2] is, like all his lives, a miscellaneous ragbag of information, some reliable, some not, arranged by topics; he takes no interest in wars and very little in constitutional changes, and revels in personal anecdotes, and anything which reveals the character and habits of his subject. His frequent citations show that he had read the earlier historians assiduously. Plutarch[3] in composing his lives of Cicero, Brutus and Antonius made use of Valerius Messalla, Asinius Pollio and Augustus' autobiography, as his citations show. The last surviving narrative of the civil wars (down to 35 B.C.) is that of Appian,[4] an Alexandrian lawyer, who wrote under Antoninus Pius. He is supposed to have followed Asinius Pollio, but might equally have used Valerius

[1] Fragments in Peter, *op. cit.*, Vol. II. 91–8.
[2] Text and translation in the Loeb series, commentary in E. S. Shuckburgh, *Suetonius, Divus Augustus* (Cambridge, 1896).
[3] Text and translation in the Loeb series.
[4] Text and translation in the Loeb series.

Messalla or some later writer. He also describes Augustus' Illyrian wars, probably following Messalla, who fought in them.

The only full length account of Augustus' reign which has survived is contained in the History of Rome by Cassius Dio of Nicaea.[1] Dio had a long and distinguished senatorial career, culminating in a second consulship in A.D. 229. Encouraged by Septimius Severus he began collecting materials for his History in 197 and completed this preliminary task in ten years. In 207 he began to write, finishing his work in 219.

Writing more than two centuries after the events that he describes, he labours under certain disadvantages. He cannot avoid exercising hindsight, and interpreting Augustan institutions in the light of what they had become in his own day. He divides history into periods, making the monarchy spring into life complete in 27 B.C. after the Republic and the civil wars. On the other hand he has a thorough knowledge of the constitutional and administrative structure of the Empire both in his own day and in the past, and carefully, and on the whole accurately, distinguishes the two.

He was moreover a very conscientious scholar, who studied his sources thoroughly, and does not seem to have been content, like most ancient historians, to combine previous historians, but looked up archive material; this at any rate seems the most likely source for the elaborate and seemingly accurate catalogues of honours and powers successively bestowed on Augustus. But for Cassius Dio we should know very little of the constitutional growth of the Augustan principate—he is the only author so much as to mention the settlements of 23 B.C. and 19 B.C.

[1] Text and translation in the Loeb series. There is a good discussion of Dio's historical method and political views in Fergus Millar, *A Study of Cassius Dio* (Oxford and New York, Oxford University Press, 1964).

map 1: The Roman Empire in 27 B.C.

THE ROMAN EMPIRE IN 27 B.C.

❶ Dynasts of AMASEIA, CARANA, COMANA, MEGALOPOLIS and ZELIA
❷ Principality of TEUCRID

BOSPORUS

DACIA

Save

Danube

RICUM

THRACE

MACEDONIA

BITHYNIA ET PONTUS

PAPHLAGONIA

PONTUS

ARMENIA MINOR

ARMENIA

ACHAEA

ASIA

GALATIA

CAPPADOCIA

PARTHIA

Euphrates

❶

❷

SYRIA

LYCIA

CYPRUS

CRETE

ITURAEA

JUDAEA

CYRENAICA

ARABIA

EGYPT

Nile

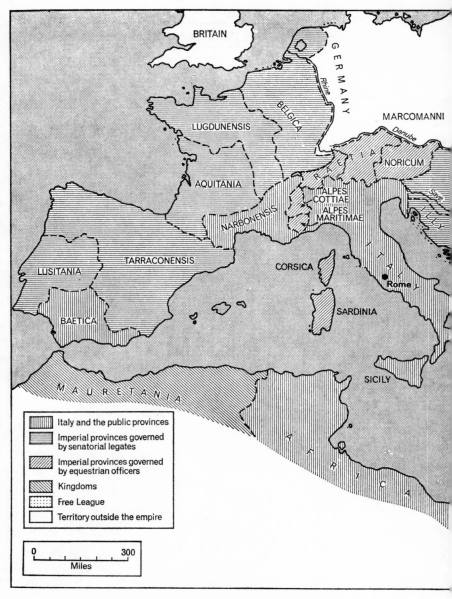

map 2: The Roman Empire in A.D. 14.

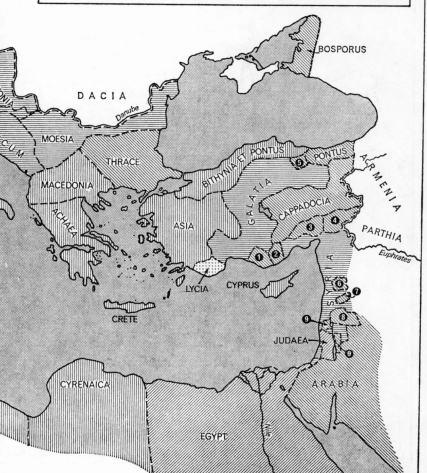

THE ROMAN EMPIRE IN A.D. 14

❶ CILICIA TRACHEIA
(attached to CAPPADOCIA)
❷ TEUCRID PRINCIPALITY
❸ TARCONDIMOTID kingdom

❹ COMMAGENE
❺ Principality of COMANA
❻ Kingdom of Emisa

❼ TETRARCHY of ABILENE
❽ TETRARCHY of PHILIP
❾ TETRARCHY of ANTIPAS

BOSPORUS

PANNONIA

DACIA

Danube

RICUM

MOESIA

THRACE

BITHYNIA ET PONTUS

PONTUS

ARMENIA

MACEDONIA

GALATIA

CAPPADOCIA

PARTHIA

ACHAEA

ASIA

Euphrates

❸
❹

❷
❶

LYCIA

CYPRUS

❻
❼

CRETE

❾
❽

JUDAEA

❾

CYRENAICA

ARABIA

EGYPT

Nile

map 3: The Roman Empire under Augustus.
*This map does not show the political divisions
of the Empire,*

for which see maps 1 and 2,
but marks places, peoples and districts
mentioned in the text.

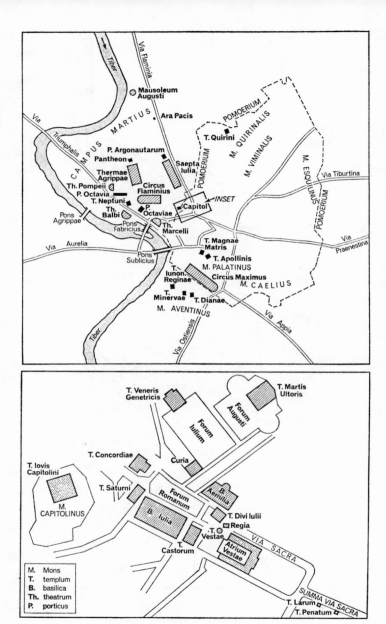

map 4: Plan of Rome.

Glossary

Aerarium (Saturni), the public treasury of the Roman people, housed in the temple of Saturn in the Forum.

Aerarium militare, the treasury founded by Augustus in A.D. 6, to pay discharge bounties to veterans.

Ala, a cavalry unit, recruited from the provincials, usually 500, sometimes 1000 strong.

Annona, the corn supply (of Rome).

Auxilia (auxiliaries), troops recruited from the provincials; see *ala*.

Auxilium, the right of a tribune of the plebs to rescue a citizen from a magistrate attempting to arrest or punish him.

Censoria potestas, the powers of a censor, i.e. to hold the census, allot citizens to tribes, classes and centuries, and revise the roll of the Senate.

Censu, see *manumission*.

Centuria praerogativa, the century, chosen by lot from the first class, which voted first in the *comitia centuriata* (q.v.).

Comitia centuriata, the assembly of the Roman people which elected the consuls and praetors, and could pass laws. It was normally presided over by the consuls, rarely—and never for elections—by a praetor. The decision was taken by the majority of centuries, and as out of 193 centuries eighteen were of *equites* (q.v.) and seventy of the first class (those with the highest property qualification), it had a strong conservative bias.

Comitia curiata, a formal assembly maintained for various ritual purposes, such as confirming adoptions. The voting units were theoretically the thirty *curiae* (brotherhoods), but actually the presiding magistrate used thirty lictors to represent the *curiae*.

Concilium plebis, the assembly of the plebs, presided over by the tribunes of the plebs, which elected the tribunes and aediles of the plebs, and passed laws (technically *plebiscita*). The voting was by tribes, territorial divisions, thirty-five in number, covering all Italy and Roman communities overseas. In this assembly the lower classes predominated.

Consilium, a group of assessors convened by a magistrate to advise him, normally when acting as a judge.

Consular, a former consul.

Cura annonae, the administration of the corn supply of Rome.

Cura morum, power to correct moral abuses, restrain luxury, etc.

Curator aedium sacrarum monumentorumque publicorum tuendorum, a commissioner to maintain temples and public monuments.

Curator locorum publicorum iudicandorum, a commissioner to adjudicate on boundary disputes between state property and private property.

Cursus honorum, the series of magistracies, to be held in a fixed order and at statutory

AUGUSTUS

Cursus honorum—cont.
minimum ages and intervals, up to the consulate. Only the quaestorship (minimum age twenty-five) and the praetorship (minimum age thirty) were obligatory, but the vigintivirate (q.v.) was normally held before the quaestorship and the aedileship or tribunate of the plebs between the quaestorship and praetorship.

Decemviri stlitibus iudicandis, a board of ten, part of the vigintivirate (see *cursus honorum*). Their duties were judicial.

Decuria, a panel from which jurors in the criminal courts and judges for civil cases were drawn.

Denarius, the standard silver coin, equal to four sesterces or sixteen asses.

Dictator, in the early and middle Republic a magistrate with unrestricted powers, nominated by the consuls in an emergency; he held office for six months only. Sulla (82–79 B.C.) and Caesar (49–44 B.C.) revived the office in a new form, holding it for years together, and using it to make constitutional changes.

Equester ordo, equites, see pp. 136–9.

Filius familias, a son under *patria potestas* (q.v.).

Fiscus, literally 'basket', a deposit for money, public or private. In the later principate the term was used for the imperial treasury and financial administration as opposed to the *aerarium*, the state treasury. In Augustus' day the term appears to be used for the emperor's privy purse and for provincial treasuries, where public money deriving from the taxes was kept before it was paid out for local expenditure or remitted to the *aerarium*.

Imperium, the powers held by a consul, praetor or dictator. They included military command, jurisdiction, civil and criminal, the right to summon the Senate and elicit *senatus consulta* (q.v.), the right to summon the assembly of the people and hold elections and propose laws. Proconsuls held a similar *imperium* within their provinces, but it naturally comprised only military command and jurisdiction.

Imperium consulare, the *imperium* of a consul, which was superior to that of a praetor.

Imperium maius, a superior *imperium*, e.g. of a dictator over a consul, or a consul over a praetor. A holder of *imperium maius* could issue prohibitions or orders to holders of lesser *imperia*.

Imperium proconsulare, the *imperium* of a proconsul, operative only in his province.

Imperium pro praetore, imperium with the rank of a praetor.

Infamia, an official mark of disgrace, which involved certain legal disabilities.

Inter amicos, see *manumission*.

Iudex quaestionis, the president of a criminal court (*iudicium publicum*, q.v.) who was not a praetor. He was normally an ex-aedile.

Iudicium publicum, also called *quaestio*, a criminal court presided over by a praetor or *iudex quaestionis* (q.v.), with a jury of *iudices* (see pp. 124–7).

Latus clavus, the broad purple stripe on their tunic worn by senators (see pp. 91–2).

Magister equitum, the second in

GLOSSARY

command of a dictator, nominated by him.

Manubiae, money realized by the sale of booty. It was customary for the general to remit part to the treasury, to distribute part to his troops, and to keep part for himself. He was expected to spend his share on a public building.

Manumission, was either formal or informal. The two methods of informal manumission were either to write a letter to your slave declaring him free (*per epistulam*) or to declare him free before a group of friends (*inter amicos*). A slave so freed did not become a Roman citizen and in strict law remained a slave, but if his master tried to re-enslave him, he could appeal to the praetor, who would normally uphold his liberty. There were three means of formal manumission, which made the slave legally a free man and a Roman citizen; by will (*testamento*), by registering the slave in the census as a citizen (*censu*), and by a legal ceremony before a consul or praetor at Rome or a proconsul (and probably a *legatus Augusti* and the prefect of Egypt) in the provinces (*vindicta*).

Municipium, a self-governing town of Roman citizens which was not a colony.

Nobiles (nobles), see p. 2.

Optimates, see p. 2.

Ovatio, a victory parade inferior to a triumph.

Patria potestas, the absolute power exercised by a father over his sons (and grandsons and daughters) of whatever age, unless he formally released them. Among other things the *pater*

familias could alone hold property and whatever his sons earned or inherited went to him.

Per epistulam, see *manumission*.

Plebiscite, a law passed by the *concilium plebis* (q.v.) proposed by one or more tribunes of the plebs.

Pomoerium, ritual boundary of the city of Rome, following the line of the ancient Servian walls, which divided the civilian area within (*domi*) from the military area without (*militiae*). A proconsul, whose *imperium* was only valid *militiae*, lost it on crossing the *pomoerium*.

Pontifex, a member of the most important priestly college, numbering sixteen persons, generally nobles.

Pontifex maximus, the head of the college of *pontifices*.

Populares, see pp. 2–4.

Princeps iuventutis, leader of the equestrian order (in the narrow sense, see p. 137), a title apparently invented by Augustus for youthful heirs to the throne. The *equites* were technically *iuvenes* (fit for active military service).

Proscription, a list of persons, publicly posted, for whose death a reward was offered. The property of the victims was confiscated.

Publicani, contractors who bought from the state (by auction) the collection of a tax (*publicum*).

Quaestio, see *iudicium publicum*.

Quattuor viri capitales, a board of minor magistrates (see *vigintiviri*), who maintained the prison and executed the condemned. They normally numbered three (*tresviri*) but were temporarily raised to four by Caesar.

Quindecimviri sacris faciundis, a priestly college of fifteen members, who kept the Sibylline Books and regulated foreign cults.

Res repetundae, extortion by magistrates, usually from provincials.

Revocatio Romae, an obscure process whereby a litigant in Italy or the provinces could claim trial at Rome.

Senatus consultum, a resolution of the Senate. It had no legal force, being in form an expression of opinion or a request to a magistrate, but was normally regarded as binding.

Senatus consultum ultimum, a resolution of the Senate 'that the consuls see to it that the state takes no harm'. It was deemed to proclaim martial law and to empower the consuls to ignore the right of appeal.

Sesterce, a copper coin worth four asses, or a quarter of a denarius.

Tribunicia potestas, the powers of a tribune of the plebs to bring aid (*auxilium* q.v.) to any citizen against a magistrate, to veto any magisterial act, to convene and consult the Senate and elicit *senatus consulta* (q.v.) and to summon the *concilium plebis* (q.v.) and propose plebiscites (q.v.).

Triumph, a victory parade voted by the Senate to a consul or proconsul, praetor or propraetor, who had won a war.

Vigintiviri, a group of minor magistracies, held before the quaestorship. They comprised the *decemviri stlitibus iudicandis* (q.v.), the *tresviri capitales* (see under *quattuor viri capitales*), the *tresviri aere argento auro flando feriundo* (the masters of the mint), and the *quattuorviri viarum curandarum* (who maintained the streets of Rome).

Select Bibliography

Chapters 1–5

The reign of Augustus is very thoroughly covered in the *Cambridge Ancient History*, vol. X (Cambridge and New York, Cambridge University Press, 1934, reprinted 1966). Chapters I–IV (W. W. Tarn and M. P. Charlesworth) treat the period 44–30 B.C.; V–VI (H. Stuart Jones) the constitution; VII–VIII (G. H. Stevenson) the administration and the army; IX (J. G. C. Anderson) the Eastern frontier; X (H. I. Bell) Egypt; XI (A. D. Momigliano) Judaea; XII (R. Syme) the Northern frontiers; XIII (F. Oertel) economic developments; XIV (H. Last) social policy; XV (A. D. Nock) religion; XVI (T. R. Glover) literature; XVII (E. Strong) art. There is a final summary by F. E. Adcock (XVIII). As might be expected from the authors this is all sound stuff, some of it interesting.

T. Rice Holmes, *The Architect of the Roman Empire* (Oxford, Clarendon Press; New York, Oxford University Press, 1928), is a detailed narrative of events from 44 B.C. to A.D. 14, with full citation of the sources and a large number of appendices on controversial points. Vol. I (44–27 B.C.) is much fuller than Vol. II (27 B.C.–A.D. 14). A very useful book for verifying matters of fact. For Augustus' rise to power see John M. Carter, *The Battle of Actium; the Rise and Triumph of Augustus Caesar* (London, Hamish Hamilton, 1970).

M. Reinhold, *Marcus Agrippa: A Biography* (Geneva and New York, W. F. Humphrey Press, 1933), is a useful study of a rather enigmatic character; so is M. Hadas, *Sextus Pompey* (New York, Columbia University Press, 1930).

R. Syme, *The Roman Revolution* (Oxford, Clarendon Press; New York, Oxford University Press, 1939, reprinted 1967), is a fascinating study of the decline and fall of the Roman nobility from the last years of the Republic to the death of Augustus. Professor Syme has a curious affection for the *nobiles* and a violent prejudice against Augustus, but the picture he draws is a valuable corrective to the conventional view.

Ch. Wirszubski, *Libertas as a Political Idea at Rome during the Late Republic and Early Empire* (Cambridge and New York, Cambridge University Press, 1950, reprinting 1970), is a valuable study of political terminology as a clue to political ideas;

D. C. Earl, *The Age of Augustus* (London, Elek; Toronto, Ryerson Press, 1968), is a good popular book, lavishly illustrated.

Chapters 6–7

M. Hammond, *The Augustan Principate* (Cambridge, Mass., Harvard University Press; London, Oxford University Press, 1933; reprinting New York, Russell and Russell), a useful handbook on the constitution, with full citation of sources and literature.

G. E. F. Chilver, 'Augustus and the Constitution, 1939–1950', *Historia* 1 (1950), pp. 408–35, a discussion of the literature in this period.

E. T. Salmon, 'The Evolution of the Augustan Principate', *Historia* 5 (1956), pp. 456–78.

A. H. M. Jones, *Studies in Roman Government and Law* (Oxford, Blackwell; New York, Barnes and Noble, 1960, reprinted 1968), I. 'The Imperium of Augustus', II. 'The Censorial Powers of Augustus', III. 'The Elections under Augustus'.

Chapter 8

Jones, *Studies*, VII. 'Procurators and Prefects in the Early Principate'.

P. A. Brunt, 'Charges of Provincial Maladministration under the Early Principate', *Historia* 10 (1961), pp. 189–227.

G. W. Bowersock, *Augustus and the Greek World* (Oxford, Clarendon Press; New York, Oxford University Press, 1965), an interesting study of a neglected field.

F. Millar, 'The Emperor, the Senate and the Provinces', *Journal of Roman Studies* 56 (1966), pp. 156–66.

Chapter 9

H. M. D. Parker,, *The Roman Legions* (2 ed., Cambridge, Heffer; New York, Barnes and Noble, 1958).

G. L. Cheesman, *The Auxilia of the Roman Imperial Army* (Oxford, Clarendon Press, 1914; reprint, Hildesheim, G. Olms, 1970).

C. G. Starr, *The Roman Imperial Navy* (2 ed., Cambridge, Heffer; New York, Barnes and Noble, 1960).

Chapter 10

Jones, *Studies*, VI. 'The Aerarium and the Fiscus'.

F. Millar, 'The Fiscus in the First Two Centuries', *Journal of Roman Studies* 53 (1963), pp. 29–42.

P. A. Brunt, 'The Fiscus and Its Development', *Journal of Roman Studies* 56 (1966), pp. 75–91.

SELECT BIBLIOGRAPHY

Chapter 11

Jones, *Studies*, IV. 'I Appeal unto Caesar', V. 'Imperial and Senatorial Jurisdiction in the Early Principate'.

P. D. Garnsey, 'The Lex Iulia and Appeal under the Empire', *Journal of Roman Studies* 56 (1966), pp. 167–89.

Chapter 12

R. H. Barrow, *Slavery in the Roman Empire* (London, Methuen, 1928; reprinted 1968, also New York, Barnes and Noble).

A. M. Duff, *Freedmen in the Early Roman Empire* (1928, reprinted Cambridge, Heffer; New York, Barnes and Noble, 1958).

Chapter 13

R. M. Ogilvie, *The Romans and Their Gods, in the Age of Augustus* (London, Chatto and Windus; New York, W. W. Norton, 1970), a volume in the present series.

L. R. Taylor, *The Divinity of the Roman Emperor* (Middletown, Conn., American Philological Association, 1931).

Chapter 14

G. Williams, 'Poetry in the Moral Climate of Augustan Rome', *Journal of Roman Studies* 52 (1962), pp. 28–46.

Index

Note: Names of major figures are in capitals.

INDEX

INDEX

INDEX

INDEX

INDEX